THE MAKING OF

T2

TERMINATOR₋ 2
JUDGMENT DAY

THE MAKING OF

T2

TERMINATOR™ 2
JUDGMENT DAY

by DON SHAY and JODY DUNCAN

TITAN BOOKS

LONDON

Acknowledgments

A great many people contributed to this book. Our initial nod must go to James Cameron—who solicited our involvement—and to coproducers B.J. Rack and Stephanie Austin who opened doors and saw to it that we had unrestricted access to the set. Those whose quotes are woven into the text merit special thanks for making time to talk with us during an extremely demanding shoot. Behind the scenes, Larry Kasanoff of Lightstorm Entertainment bought us enough time to make this project a viable one, and agents Nancy Roberts and Lou Malacarne jumped in at the last minute to look out for our interests. Alexandra Drobac—assistant to the director—was always available and cheerfully helpful, as were producers' assistants Mary Lamar Mahler and Lisa Stone. Assistant production coordinators Dean Wright and Crystal Dowd responded to countless requests for information and directions. Our thanks go also to unit publicist Steve Newman and to still photographer Zade Rosenthal whose work illustrates this book— and last, but not least to Jim Brown of Cal State San Bernardino, Jeff Burdick, Anne Merrem and video documentarian Ed Marsh.

THE MAKING OF TERMINATOR 2

ISBN 1 85286 394 3

Published by
Titan Books Ltd
58 St Giles High Street
London
WC2H 8LH

First edition July 1991
10   9   8   7   6   5   4   3   2   1

CONTENTS

INTRODUCTION

"I'll be back."

It was late in the autumn of 1984 when the Terminator made that promise, standing at the front desk of a Los Angeles police precinct dubiously claiming to be "a friend of Sarah Connor's." It became the catch phrase of a film that—by its distributors, at least—had been expected to reap only a modest profit from its less-than-lavish investment.

Such low expectations were understandable. *The Terminator*, cowritten and directed by James Cameron, was only the second time out for a thirty-year-old director whose previous effort had been the unmemorable *Piranha II*. In addition, it was the first solo outing for a similarly untried producer—Gale Anne Hurd—who, like Cameron, had only recently emerged from the B-film factory of producer Roger Corman. Starring unknowns Linda Hamilton and Michael Biehn, along with Arnold Schwarzenegger in his first role outside the "muscles and loincloth" genre, the film did not seem destined to break box office records. In spite of its sensitively portrayed love story and intelligently written screenplay, *The Terminator* was summarily dismissed as nothing more than a fight-per-minute action film—a shoot-'em-up with a science fiction twist.

But with the film's release, something amazing happened. Hardcore action fans loved it. Science fiction fans loved it. Teenage boys, their fathers and their mothers loved it. Incredibly, even the critics loved it, many placing it on their year-end "ten best" lists. And the little film with the $6.5-million budget went on to become one of the biggest moneymakers of the season and the year.

In the aftermath of the *Terminator* phenomenon, Cameron went on to write and direct both *Aliens* and *The Abyss*, further cementing his reputation as a filmmaker worthy of note. However, a possible sequel to the story of Sarah Connor and the son who was destined to lead a rebel band against a computer-run army of machine warriors was never far from the director's thoughts. Numerous contractual entanglements threatened to keep the *Terminator 2* project forever in the realm of fantasy until suddenly, early in 1990, a deal was struck with Carolco Pictures and the project was a "go." The only catch was that it had to be brought in on time for a summer of 1991 release. Accepting the terms, Cameron immediately sat down with a cowriter to develop the concept that he had been contemplating for half a decade.

Terminator 2 picks up ten years after a pregnant Sarah Connor drives off into the Mexican desert. Separated from her son and incarcerated in a psychiatric hospital, Sarah is a woman who has been hardened by fear

Arnold Schwarzenegger returns as the Terminator.

Robert Patrick as the T-1000, a technologically advanced terminator sent to destroy young John Connor.

and the haunting prospect of Judgment Day—the day nuclear devastation is to be unleashed by the rogue computer Skynet, the day only she has the knowledge to foresee. John, a street-smart kid who doubts the sanity of his mother's doomsday predictions, becomes the target of a new, technologically advanced terminator—the T-1000—which is dispatched by the futuristic machine world. In response, another Terminator—the now-obsolete model originally sent to kill Sarah—has been reprogrammed by the adult John Connor and sent back in time on a mission to protect the boy. A lethal battle ensues between these two nonhuman adversaries—a cat-and-mouse game in which nothing less than humanity's survival on the planet is at stake.

Only eighteen months elapsed between the start of the screenplay and the completion and release of *Terminator 2: Judgment Day*. It would have been a too-short schedule for any major film, but was especially harrowing for one which entailed scores of hideously complex visual effects nestled among breathtaking stunts and physical effects gags enough for three films. In a super-human feat worthy of the Terminator himself, a host of talented and committed producers, designers, actors, effects artisans and technicians—all under the leadership of Jim Cameron—brought the story of the Terminator to its summation in a film of white-knuckle suspense and roller coaster action.

The Terminator is, indeed, back.

A TRUE
CONTINUATION:
AN INTERVIEW WITH
JAMES CAMERON

T2 *A sequel to* The Terminator *was a long time in coming. When did you first start thinking about the possibilities for a second story?*

Very shortly after the first film was released. It was actually Arnold who got me thinking about it—he loved the role and was interested in doing it again. But I didn't write the first film with a preconceived notion of doing a sequel. To me, *The Terminator* was a pretty self-sufficient story, even though it had a lot of side alleys that could easily be explored in a sequel. I actually shot a scene in the first film in which we saw the Terminator computer chip discovered at the factory where he was finally destroyed by Sarah—a factory which a closing shot would have revealed to be Cyberdyne Systems. There was also a scene in the first film in which Sarah gets the idea to blow up Cyberdyne so that Skynet never happens. Those scenes were cut for a variety of reasons. So even though you didn't see them in the film, all of the seeds of the current story were there in the first script. In a way, the sequel was born out of unused elements of the first story.

Once the Terminator 2 *project was given a green light, everything had to come together very quickly. Was your decision to bring William Wisher in to cowrite the script with you a function of time, or did the idea of working with a collaborator appeal to you creatively?*

It was partly a function of time and partly the fact that Bill was involved creatively with the first picture and it seemed like a natural thing to do. I knew that working with a collaborator would allow me to sort through story ideas very quickly. I didn't have the time to sit on it

The Terminator fires on police from a second-story window in the Cyberdyne Systems research lab.

and think about it for a long period—which is what I usually do when I write. Working with Bill was a good way for me to get to the basic structure of the story very quickly.

There are a lot of ways you could have gone with a sequel. What was the evolutionary process that led you in this particular direction?

It was important to me from the beginning that we do a true continuation of the story. Bill and I discussed a lot of ideas, one of which was a "two-Arnold" concept in which there would be a good terminator and a bad terminator, both played by Arnold. Two things turned me away from that concept: First, it felt gimmicky; and second, I knew that, visually, we would have had to do something to distinguish the "good" terminator from the "bad" terminator. It would have meant having Arnold in appliance makeup for the whole five months of the shooting schedule—and I didn't want Arnold Schwarzenegger cranky with me.

Do you think the 'two-Arnold' concept would have worked dramatically?

It could have. But we began to realize that if the audience was going to root for the good terminator, his adversary had to be *more* threatening and *more* powerful than he was. But then we were faced with a dilemma—

Director James Cameron confers with Schwarzenegger. Cameron had considered using Schwarzenegger in a dual role as both terminators, but ultimately rejected the notion.

Battles with the T-1000—a more advanced and lethal adversary—leave the Terminator severely battered and disfigured.

what is bigger, stronger and more terrifying than the Terminator? We couldn't just build a bigger hydraulic machine, because that would stray too far from the basic concept of the terminator as an infiltration unit. What is the point of imitating human beings if you imitate them in such a laughably noticeable manner that they no longer work as infiltrators?

Arnold doesn't exactly get lost in a crowd.

True. But if we'd gone with someone even bigger, it just would have stretched the logic too much. So we realized that we had to come up with something that was more terrifying than the Terminator, and yet didn't look any more overtly inhuman. Eventually we wound up with the idea of the T-1000. In one of the

earliest drafts of the original *Terminator*, I had actually incorporated a sort of liquid metal robot that could take any form. Then John Carpenter's *The Thing* came out—which was another shape-changing kind of monster—and so I abandoned the idea. But I never lost that image of a liquid metal endoskeleton.

What were some of the problems you foresaw in the shape-changer concept?

Stan Winston brought up the most convincing argument against it, which was that a shape-changer would be difficult for an audience to be afraid of because it really isn't a character—it could be a toaster and then a fire hydrant and then a guy walking down the street. It could be anything; and because of that, the audience would lose touch with the story's central nemesis. But then I realized that we could overcome that problem by having the T-1000 constantly reiterating a central form—something the character would always revert to in between these shape-changing excursions. So we came up with the central form of the cop—Austin. I think the audience will leave the theater with the definite impression of Robert Patrick as the character of the T-1000—that face and those eyes are behind the character, no matter what form it takes.

Another problem in previous films where a shape-changer of some type has been used is that often there are no rules that govern its physical behavior.

That's true. And if it can do anything and it is always doing new things that you didn't know it could do, ultimately you throw up your hands and say, "I can't invest in this film anymore." So we gave the T-1000 some predictable rules: It can't fly; it can't suddenly become a complex machine like a car or a jet; it can't alter its own chemical composition. All it can do is alter the color and texture of its surface so that it can *imitate* objects—but it is not really changing into that object. We had to be very clear in our own minds what the rules were, and hopefully it will be clear to the audience as well.

What were some of the other story ideas you considered?

We briefly thought of playing the whole thing in the future—or at least to play more of it in the future war. We also tried for a while to come up with a way to have Sarah get back together with Reese, through time travel or something. But that became too much like a *Back to the Future* kind of thing, where the time travel itself is part of the plotting. I liked the fact that in the first film the time travel was just a stage setter. It never really came into play as a plot point. In fact, you never even saw the time machine.

In the first draft of the Terminator 2 *script, you had an involved sequence in which the time displacement chamber was featured.*

Right, and that violated the idea of the first story, to some extent. It was very nice visually, but I began to realize that the audience was totally willing to accept the notion of a time machine without showing them what this particular time machine looked like. They would fill that in for themselves, just like they had in the first film. It was a matter of giving the audience some credit.

The natural assumption is that you cut that sequence because it would have been horrendously expensive.

And it would have been horrendously expensive.

One of the interesting things about Terminator 2 *is that even though you have both Arnold Schwarzenegger and Linda Hamilton back, they aren't really playing the same characters they played in the first film.*

They've switched roles, essentially. There is a definite and intentional psychological transference between the two characters. Sarah has become a warrior, a terminator. Her reality is in the future, in the Terminator's world; and at some level, she has said to herself: "In order to survive in that world I have to become like that creature. I have to be without emotion, without compassion and pity. Because three billion people are going to die, and if I start to think about even one of them, I will go crazy." It's what happens to the human mind when it deals with the unthinkable. We don't embrace the idea of nuclear war at an emotional level, because it's too horrible. But Sarah is forced to, and that makes her unlikable and a bit crazy. The dramatic meat of the story is her finding her way back again. That's what the movie is all about—not the shoot-'em-up chase stuff.

How did Arnold react to the shift in his character from the first film to the second?

I think it took him aback a little bit at first. I think he expected something a little more like what we'd done before, and it took him a while to see how he could do all the things he'd done on the first film but with an ironic twist on it. By the time he came to work on the picture, he had it wired. He knew exactly what the tone was. He totally understood what he needed to project at each one of the different phases of the movie.

Was there some concern that with this new Terminator character you would not be playing to the expectations of Arnold's audience?

Which audience? The *Twins* audience? The *Commando* audience? I just had to do what was dramatically right for the story. Ulti-mately, that is better than trying to pander to a specific audience. You can't try and do demographics before the fact. I was only concerned that his character be *enough* reminiscent of what he was before that we wouldn't violate the story. It was a fine line to walk—when is it violent enough to be consistent with the character, but not so violent that you begin to erode your own moral stance? If the whole thrust of the movie is the value of human life, at what point does waving guns around begin to erode that moral point? It was tricky, but I think the film walks that line successfully.

Besides the recurring characters of Sarah and the Terminator, you had two other very im-

The T-1000—in human form—fires through the shattered windshield of a helicopter. As conceived, the T-1000 was a liquid metal entity capable of changing into nearly any shape.

Sarah Connor fires on the pursuing T-1000
from the back of a commandeered SWAT van.
Linda Hamilton's return in the role was
considered crucial to the continuation
of the story.

The T-1000 stalks his prey at Cyberdyne. Intent on casting an unknown actor in the role, Cameron chose relative newcomer Robert Patrick.

portant roles to fill. What specifically were you looking for when you were casting the T-1000?

We knew it would have to be a very physical performance. There wasn't a lot of dialogue for the character, so a *lot* had to be presented to the audience through the eyes and through the body. We wanted someone who would be able to meet the considerable physical demands of the role. I also wanted someone who didn't have a lot of baggage in film— somebody that we hadn't seen play other people. The T-1000 is supposedly the only one of its kind in existence, and I wanted to support that idea by casting someone who was basically an unknown. Robert Patrick was an unknown and he had that physical ability.

After looking at hundreds of professional child actors, you cast Edward Furlong—a twelve-year-old with no previous acting experience—in the role of John Connor. How did that come about?

Our casting director had a tape of Eddie and she showed it to me because, despite the fact that he was inexperienced, there was something very interesting about him. So I looked at the tape and there was definitely a glimpse of something special there, even though he really had no idea how to act and he kind of fumbled through the scene. But after I saw him, every kid actor I met seemed fake in comparison. Even the ones I had liked before seemed fake to me. So I kept coming back to him, four or five times, and finally I said, "Let's do it."

Cameron confers with Schwarzenegger and Edward Furlong on a desert set configured as a paramilitary compound.

Edward Furlong as young John Connor.

Did you have any misgivings about handing over such a crucial role to a neophyte actor?

I was terrified to cast him. It was the single scariest creative decision of the film. The whole film, all the money and all the work and all the energy that was spent, could go right in the toilet if the character of the kid didn't work. But I gambled on Eddie because he was the only one of all the kids I saw who could create a strong emotional response in front of a camera. He was able to cry. Watching him go through some of those scenes, I would get a lump in my throat—none of the other kids had come close to eliciting that kind of emotional response. He was absolutely real, and I think that comes across on the big screen.

The Terminator is the spiritual forefather to a lot of exceptionally violent films. How do you feel about that?

I think that many of the films that have copied *The Terminator* missed the point. They made the Terminator character—or whatever their version of it was—the hero. The Terminator was never meant to be the hero of the movie. He was the enemy. He was death. But some films have glorified that character and glorified the violence that went with the character. *The Terminator* was not a gory film at all, and neither is this one. They *are* intense, but I refuse to be penalized for doing my craft successfully and giving people an intense experience. In both films, there is a lot underlying all of that action and horror. I've tried to make people think about the unthinkable— nuclear war. We have to—if we don't, we're screwed. I believe that. So if I can sugar-coat it with a big epic action thriller and get people into the theaters and get them thinking about something that they wouldn't otherwise, then maybe that does some good other than just making all of us a lot more money.

24 October 1990, Reseda, California

Something is up in this modest residential area of Los Angeles County. From the intersection of Hayvenhurst and Plummer, parked trucks and trailers fan out for blocks in all four directions. Beneath the quiet crossing is a forty-foot-wide flood control channel peopled by a hundred or so bustling film crew members in T-shirts and jeans. Tensions are running a bit high. Progress has been slow this morning.

A large black tow truck with a cracked windshield and a smashed-in front end is parked in the concrete canal. Several men work with hammers and grinding instruments to further deface it. Atop the canal is a concrete block retaining wall which guards street traffic from the fifteen-foot drop-off into the channel. Only on close inspection is it evident that the top six rows are not block concrete, but a soft plaster. A large hole has been knocked into the wall—the result of a stunt shot a week so earlier when the tow truck was rigged on cables, equipped with a dummy driver and sent careening off the top of the intersection into the canal below. White plaster dust is now everywhere.

There are cops everywhere, too. At first it is unclear whether they are actors, stuntmen, extras—or a genuine squad of Reseda's finest sent to keep things under control. Something, though, is not quite right about these men. They are all strangely similar. All are the same size. All wear the same crisp black uniform. All have the same hair color and style— though one hides a ponytail behind his otherwise regulation haircut. And then the deciding clue—all wear a nametag that says AUSTIN.

Robert Patrick is called to the set. If the other black-uniformed officers are clones, he is the original. The hair is perfect. The uniform is starched sharp. The made-up face is friendly but severe. This is T-1000. Stepping with confidence down the steep slope of the canal, Patrick confers with James Cameron. Tall and lean, with reddish-blond hair and a redder-blond beard, Cameron is as young as most of the crew—younger than some—and possessed of a nervous energy that makes his knees rock back and forth rhythmically even on those rare occasions when he can be found standing still. After conferring with Patrick, Cameron settles himself into the sideseat of a "moto-cam"—a motorcycle-camera unit—and is motored several blocks away down the length of the channel. The tow truck makes a labored U-turn in the narrow passage and rumbles off in the same direction. Most of the crew follow on foot.

At the new spot in the canal, a wrecked and burnt-out car is deposited by a giant forklift. Director of photography Adam Greenberg looks through a filter from time to time, checking some lighting problem known only to himself. Crew members are at work on the tow truck again, this time rigging a dummy steering wheel on the right side of the cab. Due to lighting considerations, the truck is going to be filmed traveling the wrong direction down the canal. The resulting film will be flopped to appear correct. Two stuntmen will be in the vehicle—a mock driver on the right and an actual driver on the left wearing a black hood to conceal his presence on camera. The functional steering wheel will be hidden by a raised dash.

The area is cleared for the shot. The tow truck—with T-1000 at the wheel—is chasing a dirtbike driven by young John Connor. A camera vehicle with two cameras in the rear will record footage of the tow truck barreling through the channel. Smaller stationary cameras have been strategically concealed along the route. Several men are positioned atop the concrete canal walls to remote-operate the small battery-powered units. First assistant director Michael Haynie instructs them to hit the ground when the truck goes by so that their presence will not ruin the shot that has taken all morning to set up.

Finally, the loud diesel engine of the tow truck is fired up. The camera truck pulls out ahead of it. Cameron, seated within, peers intently into twin video monitors that reveal what his

Cameron lines up a shot from a boom arm overlooking one of the flood control channel locations. First and second units spent nearly six weeks in the canals shooting a high-speed chase sequence.

film cameras are seeing. "Action!"

The two trucks tear off at high speed down the canal, the camera vehicle only a few feet in front of the thundering black juggernaut. As the trucks race past the stationary camera emplacements, assistant directors yell out: "Get down! Get down!" The men up top obey—all but one who leans over the edge to watch. "Goddamn it!" Haynie roars at the offender. Within seconds, it is over and the vehicles pull to a stop a hundred or so yards up the channel. There are a few

tense moments until the shot is reviewed on video playback. No problem. The coverage is fine. Time for lunch.

Cast and crew gather in front of a catering truck where tables are set up cafeteria style with spaghetti and salad. The atmosphere is more relaxed now. One good shot in the can. Arnold Schwarzenegger, in black T-shirt and long Hawaiian shorts, looks the most relaxed of all as he crosses the intersection en route to his trailer—the best-looking one on the street. A woman sitting in a

yellow Toyota in the middle of the intersection, waiting to make a left turn, does a double take as she catches sight of the unmistakable figure casually crossing in front of her car. Oblivious, Schwarzenegger keeps walking, smiling, calling out greetings to this colleague and that, finally entering his trailer, which whirs with the sound of air conditioning.

Seconds later, there he is again. Not smiling. Somehow instantly transformed, in black leather jacket and pants and don't-mess-with-me sunglasses.

Aboard a motorcycle-powered camera car, Cameron peers through a hand-held camera as he choreographs one of the complex action shots during the canal chase.

A camera truck with two cameras mounted on external platforms is readied to record the action as a large tow truck driven by the T-1000 races through the narrow channel.

Edward Furlong straddles a dirtbike mounted on a tow bar as crew members prepare for a pursuit scene in the labyrinthine canal system.

It is the Terminator. God help us. "How's it goin', Pete?" someone asks. "All right," says Schwarzenegger stunt double Peter Kent. The Terminator fills a plate with spaghetti and sits down at a red-checked table.

After lunch, camera dolly tracks are set up in the bottom of the canal in preparation for a closeup of John Connor on his dirtbike. Neophyte actor Edward Furlong is freed from the school trailer and appears on the set. A little makeup is dabbed onto his face. He takes it all in stride.

The orange and white Honda is positioned in front of the tracks. Furlong mounts the bike and listens intently to Cameron's instructions. He is to turn toward camera, out of breath and frightened, looking to see if he has lost his pursuer. Then—panic! His eyes are to widen in fear as he "sees" the black tow truck come crashing through the retaining wall of the overpass and land behind him in the canal.

Before the cameras roll, Cameron rehearses the sequence with the young actor a few times, finally straddling the motorbike and performing the reactions himself to demonstrate.

A first take is shot. Furlong looks back, breathing hard. He seems relieved. Then his eyes widen and the camera dollies quickly forward. "I'm not believin' it," Cameron says good-naturedly after the cut. He takes the child to a shady spot in the channel and proceeds to lead him in a few dozen jumping jacks. Furlong remounts the bike. The camera rolls. The boy looks back—this time the hard breathing is genuine. He looks relieved. His eyes widen in fear as the camera dollies forward. "Cut." All look to Cameron. "I'll buy that," he says.

A BOY AND HIS TERMINATOR

T2 Long before *The Terminator* was released—indeed, before the script had even been sold or filmed—Jim Cameron had begun to speculate about what a proper sequel might entail. Ending as it did with a pregnant woman driving off in a jeep into the Mexican desert to prepare herself and her soon-to-be-born child for a bleak future known only to her, *The Terminator*—more than most films—seemed not just to suggest a sequel, but to demand it.

Considering the phenomenal box office success of the film, a sequel—by Hollywood's bottom-line logic—appeared to be inevitable. Yet the project, mired in contractual entanglements, remained interminably on hold. In the ensuing years, Cameron—still intrigued with the possibilities of a second film, and hopeful that the legalities would someday be ironed out—tossed story ideas around with long-time friend and fellow screenwriter William Wisher. Wisher, who had written dialogue for a few of *The Terminator*'s early scenes and had followed the project from its inception, had more than a casual interest in the development of a possible sequel. So it was with some excitement that the writer—acting more as sounding board than collaborator—listened to his friend's ideas for a sequel that appeared destined never to be made.

Cameron's premise, hastily handwritten on a sheet of legal paper, was simple. Ten years after the events of the first film, two terminators are sent back to the late twentieth century—one to kill the young John Connor, one to protect him. "From the very beginning," said Wisher, "Jim knew that the story would be something like 'a boy and his Terminator.' He had that basic idea very early on, although there were permutations of it over the years. Logically, the second story really *had* to be about the young John Connor. If the sequel had started right on the heels of the first film, with another terminator sent to kill Sarah, it would have just been the first film all over again—except this time with a pregnant lady being chased. Jim had no interest in repeating the first film. The only reason for doing a sequel would be to tell the next part of the story."

Wisher, an established writer with both television and feature credits, was heavily involved in an unrelated project with Cameron when, suddenly in January 1990, the long-sought deal that would enable the sequel to be made was struck. The catch was that *Terminator 2* would have to come together *fast* to make a release date in the lucrative summer months of the following year. With no script in hand, and precious little time in which to write one, Cameron invited Wisher to collaborate with him on the screenplay. "Jim said: '*Terminator 2* is going to happen—do you want to write it with me? Think about it.' So I thought about it—for about three seconds—and said 'yes.' "

The Terminator and John Connor prepare for a final confrontation with the T-1000. As scripted by Cameron and cowriter William Wisher, the bond of friendship between the boy and the cyborg was one of the most important elements of the story.

The two started immediately, working ten- to twelve-hour days at Cameron's house in Beverly Hills to develop a film treatment from the bare-bones premise scribbled on the now-yellowing sheet of paper. "We'd talk and take turns at the computer keyboard," Wisher recalled. "We had separate files—Sarah at Mental Hospital; Terminator and John at Bridge; Terminator at the Mall—and we would write in those files whenever we had an idea for that particular sequence, knowing that sooner or later we'd have to put all of this stuff together."

One of the major challenges in writing the sequel was retaining the elements of the first film which had so appealed to audiences, while taking the story in a new direction. It was not an easy balance to maintain. *The Terminator*—a crossover film which had attracted more than just die-hard action fans—had been as much a love story as an action/horror/suspense film. Knowing that the ill-fated but tender romance between Sarah and Reese in the original film had been a key element in its success, the screenwriters nonetheless rejected introducing a new love interest for Sarah. "We really couldn't give her someone else, because that would dissipate the relationship that Reese and Sarah had in the first film. This was a completely different story—a story about a mother and son being reunited, a story about Sarah being re-humanized after becoming, in essence, a terminator herself. That was the story we wanted to explore in this film—Sarah's journey back, not to where she started, but to some balance and humanity." In the final version of the script, Reese appears to Sarah in a brief dream sequence—a poignant scene in which their love is reaffirmed.

Sarah's dramatic change in character—from the sweet, vulnerable, unextraordinary young woman in the first film to the bitter, hardened warrior of the second—presented the screenwriters with a troublesome problem: Would an audience like, or even *accept*, this extreme, often unlikable woman? Given that she was still the central figure in the story, it was essential that the audience care about her. "In this film, Sarah is really a less attractive character than the Terminator,"

Far different from the fresh young woman of the first film, the Sarah Connor of Terminator 2 was written as a bitter, hardened survivalist.

Wisher noted, "and we were concerned about how the audience would react to that. The way we wrote it, we were basically asking the audience to trust us, to stay with us until she came around. And that is what happens at Dyson's house—she has gone to kill him, but she finds that she cannot do it. And from that point on we see her humanity return—but our concern was whether the audience would stay with us until that happened. We took a chance that they would."

Two dream sequences—frightening glimpses into the apocalyptic future—were written, in part, to elucidate Sarah's hardened frame of mind. "Sarah is so extreme, we had to have a way to peek into her mind and see her reality if we were going to understand her. The dream sequences remind the audience of the terribly high stakes Sarah is playing for—and when we see that, then the choices she makes and the things she does suddenly are logical. We understand why she has become the way she is."

Interestingly, the character of the Terminator presented the opposite problem—how to make the unfeeling killing machine of the first film into a likable, even poignant character for the second, without alienating the Arnold Schwarzenegger fans who would come to the theater expecting a full quota of Schwarzenegger head-bashing and ass-kicking. This significant change in character was one of the central points in the script. "John tells the Terminator that he can't kill anybody," stated Wisher, "and at first he is confused—he just doesn't get it. But gradually he begins to understand, and that makes him a sympathetic character—which was essential if the ending

of the film was going to work. So now we care about him as he is standing in the steel mill, busted up into a thousand pieces. And as he stares into the pit of molten steel, the audience is upset to realize that he is going to jump in—although they know he has to. John says to him, 'Are you frightened?' And the Terminator says, 'Yes'—and then, without hesitation, he jumps into the molten steel. *That's* making a robot poignant. But to make it work, we couldn't have him go around killing people throughout the rest of the film."

In the course of the story, the Terminator's programming is altered from "read" to "write"—enabling him not just to follow orders, but actually begin to think and learn. "In order to humanize the Terminator, he had to start learning—so it is an important and dramatic moment in the story. John Connor could have done that reprogramming in the future before sending him back, but it would have given the robot the ability to think for himself and therefore alter his own program if

Her humanity restored, Sarah applies all of her courage and training to defend her son and the future of mankind from the implacable T-1000.

John says a tearful goodbye as the Terminator prepares to lower himself into a vat of molten steel. Cameron and Wisher knew that the scene would be one of the most poignant of the film.

he felt like it. That is a risk that the adult John Connor didn't want to take—and Sarah still doesn't want to take. But young John does. So this allows us a chance to pit their opposing viewpoints against each other—Sarah hates and distrusts technology; John wants to take a chance with this thing. And John wins. We see him, for the first time, make a command decision. And from that moment on, the Terminator begins to learn."

The screenwriters grappled with ethical considerations in the handling of the character of young John Connor. Though the logic of

the story mandated that the child would be familiar with firearms and skilled at using them, both Cameron and Wisher questioned the moral responsibility of incorporating scenes that would depict the young boy brandishing weapons. "We really had to feel our way through that problem," admitted Wisher. "What we came up with finally was John's indifference to guns—he knows about them, but they hold nothing for him. There are no scenes where John starts blowing people away. We thought at one point that we might have to have scenes where he threatens people with weapons or something, but we ultimately realized that even that would be too much—the kid and guns just wasn't going to fly. But it also made sense that Sarah would want him to carry one, so we wrote a scene where Sarah tries to give him a gun and John refuses to take it. And that's how we explain this gun-savvy kid not carrying one."

As scripted, the gun-savvy kid, his slightly whacked-out mother and the Terminator with the newly raised consciousness are pitted against the formidable and seemingly indestructible T-1000—a liquid metal entity of highly advanced technology that can change instantly into any shape it has sampled by touch. The concept of the "shape-changer" as the ultimate infiltration unit had first captured Cameron's imagination when he was in the earliest stages of writing *The Terminator.* Because of budgetary concerns, however, he

had opted for a more traditional kind of robot in the first film—but the idea of the shape-changer stuck, and eventually was resurrected for *Terminator 2.*

Though the shape-changer was always the favored concept for the film's new villain, Cameron and Wisher explored other possibilities as well. One was Arnold Schwarzenegger playing a dual role as both the good terminator and the bad terminator. "The biggest disadvantage of that idea was that the bad terminator wouldn't be any bigger or any more deadly than Arnold—because it would *be* Arnold—so where was the threat? Another idea we kicked around was that of a female terminator—kind of an 'Arnold versus the Bitch' idea. But that seemed almost comical. So we came back to the original concept of the shape-changer."

Throughout most of the film, the T-1000

Though John Connor is tough and wise beyond his years, the screenwriters felt ethically bound to avoid scenes in which the youth was required to brandish weapons.

The T-1000 in his guise as an inconspicuous cop. The slight-statured police officer created a sharp—and intentional—contrast to the brute strength of the original Terminator.

appears in the "shape" of a police officer—one of its first modern-day victims. As conceived by Cameron and Wisher, the police officer form of the T-1000 was to be unimpressive in size and inconspicuous in appearance. "I really liked the fact that the T-1000 was smaller than the Terminator," Wisher said. "He's a normal-size guy, and yet you can't kill him. It says something interesting in the film, I think—'You know all those muscles you've got? Well, they're not going to work this time.' The thing that the original Terminator did best is almost useless against this thing; because if you punch it, it just moves out of the way. So now the Terminator has to strategize a little bit, which is a tougher challenge and more interesting."

Finding a way to kill the T-1000, in fact, became one of the toughest challenges for the screenwriters as well. "We really struggled with that. We had set up the physical rules for how this thing worked: If you blow it up, it will form back together; if you blow it up over a large area, it will just take a longer time to come back together. You could cut it into five pieces and ship each piece to a different continent and you'd be safe probably for your lifetime—but eventually, that thing would reform. We finally decided that the only way to stop it would be to physically alter the alloy—mix it with something else that would change its molecular structure. One of my early ideas was that it would get melted down and turned into a set of Kraftsman tools, which was a fun metaphor—technology as something that can work for you or against you. We both liked the idea, but it never quite worked. We finally settled on the idea of the steel plant,

1.

Storyboards for a sequence at the Pescadero State Hospital for the Criminally Insane in which the T-1000 transforms from the checkered flooring of the lobby into his quasi-human form. All of the 'morphing' scenes were realized by computer generated imagery created at Industrial Light and Magic.

2.

3.

1.

2.

3.

The Terminator assists Sarah and John as they escape from the overturned SWAT van at the height of the freeway chase. Sarah's initial distrust of the cyborg eventually gives way to respect and gratitude.

which was one of those things born of necessity—dropping into a vat of molten steel was the only way we could think of to kill the thing."

Four weeks after first sitting down to write, Cameron and Wisher had a completed forty-page treatment. Though no dialogue had yet been written, every element of the story was in place. "It was all there—the action and the scenes and the specific shots. The only thing missing was the dialogue, which—if you are any good at it at all—is not the hard part. The hard part is making sure that the story works, that everything is motivated properly and that it is exciting and interesting." The treatment was divided between the two writers—Wisher taking the first half and Cameron the second—so that each could work separately on fleshing out the narrative and writing the dialogue that would comprise the finished screenplay. After one or two days of solitary work, the two would meet to read what each had written, making comments and suggestions for rewrites. This process continued for another four weeks until finally a first draft of the screenplay was realized.

In its first-draft form, the script was not only too long but would have been prohibitively expensive to produce. "It would have been a $200-million movie," said Wisher. "So we had to go in and tighten up on things that were obviously going to cost a lot. For example, any time the T-1000 changed his shape, we knew that was going to be a lot of money. So we would look at certain moments in the script and say, 'Do we really need the shot of him picking up the cup of coffee and turning into it?' If it wasn't essential, we had to cut it."

Length was another factor in cutting the script. One major sequence was trimmed considerably and another was completely deleted in an effort to shorten the screenplay to a reasonable page count. The deleted sequence took place at Salceda's desert encampment, where Sarah had presumably gone to learn her survival skills. Returning to the camp, Sarah seeks the help of an ex-marine mercenary who had been her teacher. Though they were interesting and contributed much to Sarah's character development, both the scene and the mercenary were deleted from the final script.

Though not excised entirely, the future war sequence at the beginning of the film was shortened to a mere fraction of its original length. Among the cuts was a revealing scene between the adult John Connor and his father, Kyle Reese. "It was their good-bye scene—the scene Reese talked about in the first film but you never saw—where John sends Reese back in time. It was a very poignant kind of scene—the son saying good-bye to the father. And Reese, of course, doesn't *know* that he is his father. John knows he is sending Reese to his death and he is trying not to let that show. Then Reese steps into this time transference machine and he is gone. One of the soldiers asks John, 'What happens to him?' And John says, 'He goes to L.A.; he completes his mission; he's killed—and he's my father.' Then they go into another room where there are rows of dormant terminators and they all look like Arnold—but there is one missing, which is the one from the first film. It was a wonderful scene—the kind of thing a writer really misses, but an audience never will."

In only a little more than two months, Cameron and Wisher had completed a tight and polished screenplay for *Terminator 2*—a screenplay which, rather than rehashing the original, sought to bring the story of *The Terminator* to a logical and satisfying conclusion.

"*The Terminator*, to me, was a perfect movie," Bill Wisher concluded. "It sounds funny, but I think *The Terminator* is very much like *It's a Wonderful Life*—it's a story that says your life could make a difference. On the surface you're nobody, but you *could* be the most important person in the world. People can't help but love that kind of story. *Terminator 2* is very different and, in a lot of ways, it is not as lean and perfect a story. It is bigger and it asks more complicated questions. And it is risky, because it does things that people are not going to expect in a sequel. We didn't take the easy way with *Terminator 2*—which could prove to have been a mistake. But if it works, we'll turn out to be geniuses."

5 November 1990, San Jose, California

The air is cold and damp, as it most often is at night in Fremont, a suburb of San Jose in the heart of the Silicon Valley. Powerful lights mounted on cranes illuminate a sleek, three-story glass and steel edifice in the middle of a high-tech industrial park. The triangular black and white logo on the front of the building reads CYBERDYNE SYSTEMS.

Second-story windows have been blasted out the previous night. In the empty frame of one stands the Terminator holding a MAC 10 machine gun, stretching and yawning as he waits for the cameras to roll. From the ground, it is impossible to tell if this is Schwarzenegger or a stunt double. The precariousness of his position on the window ledge, however, suggests the latter.

A dozen Los Angeles police cars, lights ablaze, have pulled in front of the building. A large black SWAT van is also in evidence, and a dozen men in black SWAT team regalia are among the two hundred or so people who swarm in front of the building.

Behind the building sit the requisite trailers and trucks that house personnel and equipment. A City of Fremont fire truck stands ready also. Five firemen sit huddled near the truck, drinking coffee and watching a small TV, ready to jump into action if the blasting and pyrotechnics of the night's shoot should go awry. Sarah, John and the Terminator have convinced scientist Miles Dyson that his top-priority project must be destroyed to preserve the future of humanity. But Cyberdyne security forces and area police take exception to the commando tactics they are employing to ensure its happening. There will be major fireworks.

The rear of the building is open, revealing a two-story warehouselike interior which belies the finished look of the exterior. The third "story" is merely a facade of glass installed by the art department days earlier. No offices or finished walls or corridors are to be found inside this shell—only a carpeted and decorated foyer constructed for shots of the SWAT team entering the building. Interior scenes will be filmed later, hundreds of miles away at a studio in Valencia, California.

Lights have been positioned to perfection. Trees in front of the building have been hastily trimmed to afford a better camera angle. Cameras are finally ready to roll. At some command heard only by those on headset, everything begins to happen at once. A police helicopter flies into the scene and hovers near the top of the building. The Terminator opens fire on the army of police below. Fire erupts behind him and smoke billows out from the open window frame. All hell breaks loose on the ground floor, uniformed men drawing weapons and squatting behind squad cars. The sounds of heavy fire split the quiet night for several seconds. Then, just as suddenly, it is over.

There are whoops and hollers of appreciation for the spectacle from the two hundred or so onlookers who have lined up on the street that faces the building across a wide field. Looking like the early arrivals on a parade route, some have brought lawn chairs; some sit on bales of hay removed from the back of a pickup. Some have brought small children and babies bundled up against the damp cold; one or two have come prepared with binoculars and thermoses of coffee. "Have you seen Arnold yet?" asks a teenage boy joining a group of friends. A minute later, an aging farmer in overalls parks his truck, pulls up a chair and says, "Well, where is he? Where's Arnold?"

Young and old, all have come to see Schwarzenegger—even if only from a quarter of a mile away.

Police gather to rout the intruders who have penetrated the Cyberdyne research center. A third-story glass facade was added to an existing two-story structure by the production crew.

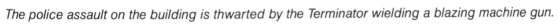

The police assault on the building is thwarted by the Terminator wielding a blazing machine gun.

MAKE IT LOOK COOL

T2 Among the first creative team members to be signed on the film was conceptual artist Steve Burg. Like cowriter Bill Wisher, Burg had been working with Jim Cameron on another project when the *Terminator 2* deal fell into place. All priorities were immediately refocused. The screenplay was still in its formative stages, but with principal photography slated to begin in October—a scant six months away—the designing of the film became an urgent and pressing matter. Burg, who had impressed Cameron enormously with his nonterrestrial concepts for *The Abyss*, was given the task of devising the futuristic sets and war machines that would be needed for the opening sequence.

Without a script to guide him, Burg had to rely on verbal descriptions gleaned from numerous conversations with the director. It was far from a blank slate situation, however. "Jim had all of the ideas in his head," Burg recalled. "I'd go over to his house and we'd talk about those ideas; and then I'd disappear for a week or so and do a lot of drawings and sketches. Jim likes to fill an entire wall with drawings, then sit back and look at all of them and decide what he likes. Because it was so early in

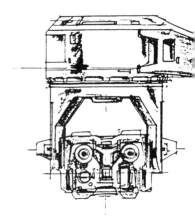

Working from James Cameron concepts used in The Terminator, *artist Steve Burg prepared refined drawings of the futuristic Hunter-Killer machines needed for the sequel.*

the process, his ideas had not completely solidified yet; so he was very open. He gave me a lot of leeway—at least at the beginning. By the end, he is always so sure of what he wants that he won't divert from the drawings one bit."

Burg concentrated his earliest efforts on designing the time displacement chamber in which Kyle Reese is sent back to the year 1985 to protect Sarah Connor. Referred to in the original film, but never seen, the farewell scene between Reese and the adult John Con-

nor was to culminate the extensive future war sequence which was planned for the *Terminator 2* prologue. Though eventually cut for budgetary reasons, the sequence as originally conceived was to depict humankind's victory over the machine world, the "dying" of the war machines and, finally, the rebels' entrance into the time displacement chamber which they find has already been used to transport a terminator back to 1985.

Cameron had definite ideas about how he

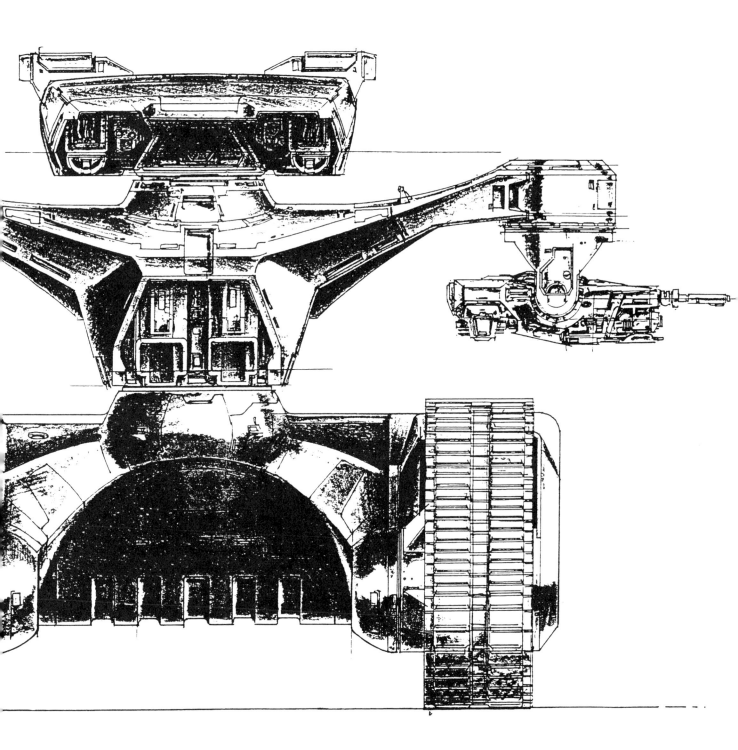

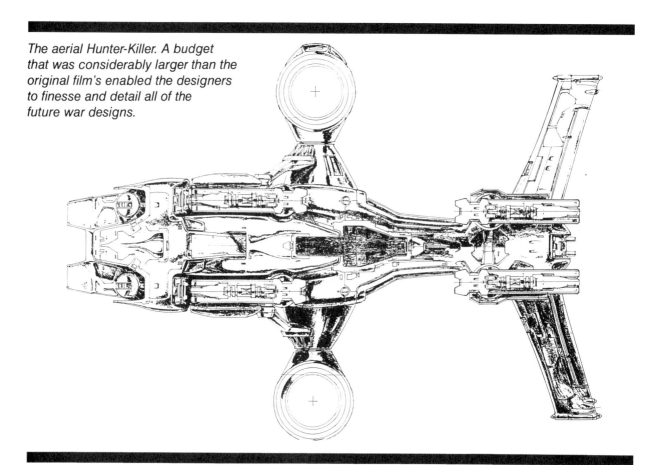

The aerial Hunter-Killer. A budget that was considerably larger than the original film's enabled the designers to finesse and detail all of the future war designs.

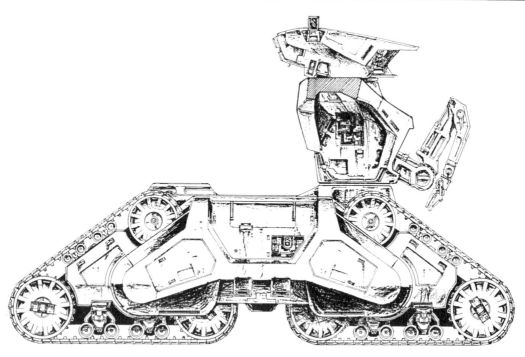

A side view of the Hunter-Killer tank. Both ground and aerial war machines were built in miniature and photographed by Fantasy II.

wanted the time displacement chamber to look. "Jim wanted something that would really knock people's socks off," Burg related. "He wanted it to be huge and powerful—something obviously inhuman. And he wanted to suggest a sense of danger as Reese got into it—as if there was so much energy there, it might just fry the hell out of him. Jim always said that it should look like it took all of the energy on the planet just to send one person back in this thing, so it had to be a very big deal."

Keeping Cameron's directives in mind, Burg designed a grand chamber that included three metallic, concentric rings suspended over a bottomless pit ten feet in diameter. As conceived, Reese would step inside the rings, which would then begin to spin faster and faster until the entire chamber split open to reveal an even larger structure surrounding it. Energy-spewing "guns" resembling X-ray machines would be directed at the minuscule human for several moments until, finally, there would be a flash of blinding light, the rings would slow to a halt, the chamber would close up—and Reese would be gone.

Reese's departure was to be followed by the discovery of the "terminator room"—a freezer chamber where scores of cyborgs are kept in suspended animation. "The way Jim saw the scene, a huge door with ice falling off of it would open and then a bunch of guys with flashlights would go in and discover the terminators. It was to be a giant room, filled with dozens and dozens of terminators hanging from piping in a kind of assembly line. There was an overhead rail system that would move them into the outer area where they would supposedly be heated up and revived and then programmed."

Though both the time travel and the terminator chamber sequences were cut during preproduction, a somewhat abbreviated version of the future war was retained. Various war machines—including those depicted in the original film—were required for the sequence. Of the new machines designed by Burg for the sequel, only the Centurion—a crablike walking machine—would make it to the final shooting script. Ultimately, however, even it was cut in subsequent efforts to con-

serve time and resources. Burg also refined the design of the fully automated "Hunter-Killer" tanks and aircraft that had been featured in *The Terminator*. "Time and money had been limited in the first film and, as a result, these machines had not been as detailed as Jim would have liked. So, for *Terminator 2*, I just tried to get them closer to an ideal."

In all of the war machine designs, appearance took precedence over mechanical integrity. "Structurally, some of these things don't make a lot of sense," Burg admitted. "But they look good. Jim's prime directive was 'make it look cool.' So I didn't concern myself too much with whether these things would actually work. My main objective was to come up with shapes that would evoke a feeling, that would make an immediate impression. That was more important than working out a function for every little thing."

By August, Burg had completed the future war designs. With production designer Joseph Nemec III already on the job orchestrating the overall design requirements of the film, Burg—along with Phillip Norwood and John Bruno—turned to storyboarding the numerous effects and action sequences. Norwood, in particular, concerned himself with defining the look of the T-1000 as he changed from one shape to another. "We decided that whenever it changed, it had to go through an intermediate chrome stage first," explained Burg. "It had to return to its 'absolute' shape. But we struggled with what that might look like. It was a very difficult thing to draw." Although all three men contributed to the storyboarding process, it was Norwood who took the often sketchy renderings and produced the polished panels that would set the overall visual style for the sequences involved.

Most of the sequences were planned and executed on video before the final storyboards were done. Such "videomatics" had been employed previously by Cameron to plot the complex submersible chase and other sequences in *The Abyss*. For *Terminator 2*, the technique proved once again to be invaluable. "Jim figured out how to execute these sequences by videotaping models with a little two-inch video camera," noted Bruno. "It was

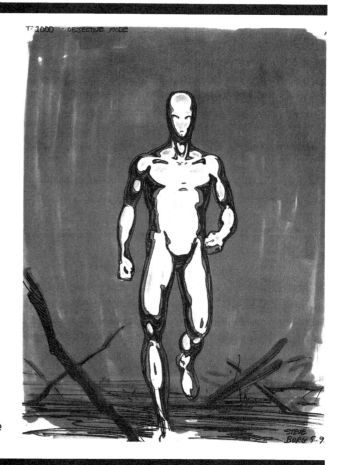

A conceptual illustration by Phillip Norwood of the T-1000 in liquid metal form.

basically a remote lens connected to a VCR which enabled him to shoot the models, experimenting with camera angles, and then print out black-and-white stills on a video printer. From those stills, we were able to draw precise, well-planned storyboards. Considering the number of effects and action shots in the film, the video approach was very helpful. We put in a lot of time on it, but we knew that anything we could do during pre-production would pay off later on—once you are on the set, there is no time to experiment."

One action scene that was choreographed using the video technique had the Terminator leaping on top of a liquid nitrogen truck, and then, as it flips over, riding it, surfer-style, as it slides on its side and crashes. "We bought the biggest tanker truck model we could find," explained Bruno, "which was about two-and-a-half feet long. Then we made up a four-inch clay model to represent Arnold. We positioned the models and shot them with the little video camera, playing with the angles and getting everything worked out—how the truck should hit, how it should flip, where Arnold could jump off and so on. So it was all figured out, every single frame, every cut, in advance."

While work on the storyboards progressed, Joe Nemec—another veteran of *The Abyss* whose work as an art director had convinced Cameron that he was capable of spearheading the entire production design—was overseeing the conceptualization and, eventually, the construction of the various location and studio sets. These included the future war environment, the psychiatric hospital in which Sarah is incarcerated, interior and exterior settings depicting the Cyberdyne headquarters and the massive steel mill in which the

TC
3

PROCESS
(handwritten, illegible)

192 D.1

PAN WITH
TANKER AS
IT SCRAPES
TOWARD
THE STEEL
MILL

cont

cont

Chase sequence storyboards depicting a tanker truck as it flips onto its side and slides into the steel mill. The action was carefully choreographed using model vehicles and a small video camera.

final showdown between the Terminator and the T-1000 takes place.

The ruins of a demolished steel plant in Fontana, California provided the backdrop for the burnt-out, war-ravaged setting of the future war. "There were mounds of firebrick at the site," recalled Nemec, "and hundred-foot-tall furnaces which had toppled over. So, especially at night and in certain light, there were some very bizarre forms out there. We added a lot of things of our own—including truckloads of stuff from the remains of the Universal Studios backlot fire that occurred while we were shooting. John Lucky, my art director, was over there one day and he called me from the lot and said, 'I'm sitting here in the middle of our future war.' It was a great idea. We dashed around like a couple of kids in a toy store and found twenty-foot-long rows of burnt bicycles and trucks, burnt balcony railings, misshapened steel and corrugated metal—things that would have been very hard to find. Then we added old streetlight posts and traffic signal standards and concrete park benches to the set. We had a good variety of things to shoot."

The Lake View Medical Center in the San Fernando Valley north of Los Angeles—which had been significantly damaged by an earthquake shortly after being built in the early 1970s and consequently has been used as a filming location ever since—was refurbished by Nemec's crew to create the sterile, inhospitable Pescadero State Hospital for the Criminally Insane. "Our concept for the hospital was to make it as cold and frightening as possible," said Nemec. "So we painted everything white—even the wire mesh in the windows. We also did a lot of construction there. All of the doors had to be changed and we had to build the night nurse's station as well as the security area. There was quite a lot of work involved to remake the medical center to the film's specifications."

Sites in both northern and southern California—also Houston and Dallas—were scouted in the search for an appropriate building to act as the exterior of the Cyberdyne headquarters. Finally, an empty two-story glass and steel structure was located in the outskirts of San Jose, California. "We had

Los Angeles in the year 2029. Human commandos crawl among the ruins in the course of a deadly future war pitting men against machines. A conceptual drawing by Steve Burg.

THE LAST ARMY - LOS ANGELES 2029

hoped to find at least a three-story building," Nemec commented, "but when we couldn't, we had to settle for adding a third-story glass facade to two sides of the building in San Jose. The glass windows were just held in place by wooden scaffolding covered with a black backdrop. The most difficult part of it was matching the unusual blue tint of the building's original windows. We never did match it exactly; but with the right lighting and shot at the right angles, you couldn't tell."

Except for the lobby and specific corridors built inside the empty building at the location site, the majority of the sets for the Cyberdyne interior were constructed at the Ventura Studios. Consisting of a security area, reception area, laboratory, vault and "clean room"—the sterile area in which microchips are produced—the sets were modeled after an

actual computer software designing facility that Nemec had toured. "It helped tremendously to get a look at that kind of artificial intelligence environment. I also looked through architectural publications I keep in files at home to get ideas for reflective surfaces and different kinds of hard surfaces. Once we locked into those ideas, we began more specific designing and model building, bringing Jim in to make sure that we were correctly interpreting the areas called for in the script."

By far the most ambitious set requirement was the refurbishment of a massive steel plant located adjacent to the future war setting found in Fontana. Dormant for seventeen years—though on occasion used by film companies for a variety of purposes—the plant required a great deal of modification and con-

Portions of the tanker truck crash were shot in miniature. Fantasy II crew members prepare the overturned quarter-scale vehicle for its slide into the steel mill.

A battered Terminator lowers himself into a vat of molten steel. The addition of the fiery 'death pit' to the abandoned steel mill location was just one of many refurbishments accomplished by the art department.

struction to make its neglected interior look like a still-functioning steel plant and to facilitate the specific action called for in the script.

Just planning the refurbishment—using a number of small-scale models—took nearly eight weeks. Two main areas of the plant were to be utilized: an open expanse on the first floor where the tanker truck crashes into the building, and an upper level where the Terminator and the T-1000 engage in a battle to the death.

In the allotted five-week construction schedule, Nemec and his crew not only cleaned and renovated those areas of the plant but also built half a dozen platforms to serve as additional acting and stunt areas. In addition, a large conveyor unit and two ladles fourteen feet in diameter and weighing nearly a thousand pounds apiece were constructed.

The ladles were built to the exact specifications of authentic ladles used for pouring molten steel. Framed first in wood, the ladles were then bound with steel rings to retain their essentially circular shape. A foam material was built up around the lip to simulate the look of metal impurities that had gathered and solidified around the spout. Out of that spout, an orangish-colored "pour" simulating

molten steel was constructed in Fiberglas. When lit properly, the Fiberglas form would create the core of molten steel. Richard Mula—who had engineered some breakthrough underwater lighting for *The Abyss*—was enlisted to produce the high-output illumination needed to simulate the white-hot liquid metal.

From the first conceptual sketches to the completion of the last set, realizing the unique look of *Terminator 2* was a year-long process that demanded the best from literally dozens of artists and craftsmen. Having worked for Cameron before, Joe Nemec, in particular, had come onto the project fully aware of the challenges it would present. "My first response after reading the script was exhaustion," Nemec recalled. "There was just so much there; and since Jim is a perfectionist, I knew he would want it all done absolutely first-rate. But he is wonderful to design for. He has been an art director himself; so, unlike some directors, he understands that side of filmmaking. And he shoots everything you build. When you know someone is going to film everything, it motivates you to do that extra bit of detail. Jim will shoot one hundred ten percent of it—and that is very rewarding."

The Terminator in front of a thousand-pound ladle constructed by the film company. Intense backlighting on an orangish-colored fiberglass core created the illusion of molten steel being poured.

15 November 1990, Long Beach, California

A two-and-a-half-mile section of the Terminal Island Freeway has been closed for filming. Crew members walk back and forth across the expanse of dirt separating the Anaheim Street on-ramp—which has been cordoned off as a production staging area—and the oddly deserted four-lane freeway a hundred yards beyond. Five blinding light towers illuminate the area. The only "traffic" on this freeway at the moment is a water truck parked beneath the Pacific Coast Highway overpass. Two helicopters with Los Angeles Police Department markings sit on the dirt field.

Jim Cameron is out in the area talking to helicopter stunt pilot Chuck Tamburro. They are about to do a dry run of their big shot for the evening. It is toward the end of the film and T-1000, at the helicopter controls, is chasing a SWAT vehicle driven by the Terminator with John and Sarah in the rear. Although it had not originally been on the schedule, Tamburro has suggested that during the low-level chase he fly his helicopter *under* the freeway overpass— an area only two lanes wide and a scant twenty feet high. The dry run is to determine the feasibility of the stunt. Two paramedics seated on a gurney near their ambulance are a reminder to one and all of the potential danger. Tamburro is confident.

The helicopter lifts off from the field and makes a sweep to the far side of the overpass. The freeway is wetted down to keep dust from kicking up and endangering the low-flying aircraft. Only Cameron and one or two others stand in the dirt field now; everyone else has gathered behind the chain link fence that runs along the side of the on-ramp.

At the word from Cameron, the helicopter approaches the overpass only a few feet off the ground and eases through. For the few moments that the helicopter takes to traverse four lanes of overhead traffic, the difficulty of the stunt is apparent—the whirling rotor blades are no more than eight feet from the concrete bridge abutments. The helicopter emerges safely and rises to a more comfortable altitude. Cameron lifts a fist in an exuberant signal of success. There is clapping and cheering from the crew. Tamburro lands the chopper close to Cameron's position on the field. After conferring with the pilot, the director quickly marches back to the on-ramp. "That's not something you see every day, is it?" he says excitedly.

Now it is time to do it again— for the cameras. Camera equipment is loaded onto trucks and transported to various vantage points along the freeway. Two tripod-mounted cameras are erected on the sloped embankment on the approach side of the overpass. Small remote-operated cameras are hidden around and beneath it. The shot will be well covered. No one wants to do it more than once.

When everything is ready, twenty cars that have been parked along the chain link fence move out onto the freeway. All are driven by stunt people, there only to provide background traffic for the shot. The black SWAT van appears on the freeway, too. For several minutes the cars sit lined up on either side of the center divider, waiting for "action" to be called. Finally, the helicopter jockeys once again into position, car lights are turned on and the column of vehicles starts moving down the highway. Because the shot will be "undercranked" to suggest greater speed, the cars travel at only thirty miles per hour. Suddenly the black van comes through the underpass, moving faster than the cars—followed closely by the helicopter, which in turn is being chased by a camera truck. The rear of the van is open and a woman inside opens fire on the chopper. Machine gun bursts split the night air as the helicopter presses to within a scant few feet of the van and its occupants. Then a quarter-mile down the freeway the chopper veers off, the van brakes to a stop and the traffic slows to a rush-hour crawl. The sequence has gone off without a hitch.

For identifiably close shots of Robert Patrick at the controls of a low-flying helicopter engaged in a perilous freeway chase, a mockup aircraft was suspended from a crane arm attached to a moving flatbed truck.

PUTTING OUT FIRES, DAY TO DAY

T2 In his first-time capacity as producer on one of his own films, Jim Cameron recognized that he would need some strong production support to manage the day-to-day details of a sprawling multimillion-dollar action and effects picture. Selected as coproducers were B.J. Rack and Stephanie Austin. With a background in production management and effects, Rack had just come off *Total Recall* as effects producer and was developing a major science fiction film at Carolco when *Terminator 2* was offered to her as an interim alternative. Austin, likewise, had a comprehensive production background and was recommended to Cameron on the strength of a television movie she had recently produced for Carolco.

The prospect of mounting and completing *Terminator 2* in time for its predetermined release date was a daunting one. "The most terrifying thing was reading the script and realizing that what we had there was about three movies," said Rack. "Not that it wasn't cohesive, but there was just so much action, one scene after another of phenomenal scale—it never stopped. So the first fear was, 'How are we going to do this movie with only three months of preproduction and one hundred shooting days and three months of postproduction?' It was overwhelming."

In the three months allocated for preproduction, the usual filmmaking requirements had to be met: the casting of major and minor roles, the scouting and selection of shooting locations and the design and construction of specific sets. In addition, there were major visual effects to be assigned, elaborate physical effects and stunts to be planned, plus extensive makeup and puppet requirements. With much to do and little time in which to do it, Cameron and his coproducers began a stint of sixteen-hour days and seven-day weeks that would last until the film was ready to shoot—and beyond.

Partly because both Cameron and Rack had extensive experience in effects, the designing and planning of the visual effects was a more thorough affair than what is traditionally attempted during preproduction. "We planned all of them up front," said Rack, "rather than doing what is typical on pictures, which is to shoot the live-action and then try to retrofit the visual effects into that. Jim is extraordinarily visual and very clear on what he wants to see and how he wants to see it. He can say, 'I see this on a 20mm lens at eighteen frames per second and the frame line ends right here and the shot should be four-and-a-half seconds.' And when it's all done, it is exactly four-and-a-half seconds. It's amazing. Planning all of these effects shots was a horrendous process—I thought we'd never get through it. We had a team of artists working around the clock. Jim would go from one guy to the next guy to the next guy, giving his input and, sometimes, grabbing it out of an artist's hand and drawing it himself. I'd never seen anything like it."

Bidding out the effects was simplified to some degree by the extensive preparation. "We pretty much put prices on everything before we took it to the effects houses," Rack explained. "Usually you show them conceptual sketches and then they go off for three months and come back with their own breakdown—but we'd already done that. We dictated the techniques and completely designed everything so that when we gave it out to bid, it was a simple matter."

Eventually, three facilities were enlisted to produce the required one hundred fifty visual effects shots. Complex miniature effects and opticals were divided between Fantasy II and 4-Ward Productions, while Industrial Light and Magic was assigned the computer-generated imagery required to change the T-1000 from one shape to another.

Just as the effects sequences had been planned and broken down, each action sequence was worked out in advance. "We tested everything we possibly could," said Rack, "shooting either with a 16mm camera or on video. For each action sequence we'd make lists of everything we had to build, everything that had to be tested, down to every detail. So we were prepared for just about every gag in the movie, which is unusual. The hours were long, but once we got into shooting, the yield was tremendous."

Casting was another concern. Though two of the major characters—Sarah and the

Schwarzenegger and Furlong prepare for a scene at the steel mill site.

Terminator—were obviously precast from the prior film, the key roles of the T-1000 and young John Connor had to be filled. Working with casting director Mali Finn, the filmmakers tested dozens of actors from all over the country.

With Hamilton and Schwarzenegger in the major roles, the producers did not have to concern themselves with casting a name actor in the role of the T-1000. "We didn't really have to worry about box office," said Austin, "so the possibilities for the T-1000 were endless. Jim shot video screen tests of various actors playing scenes and spent a lot of time going over them. It was a substantial search."

The role of the T-1000—the technologically superior killing machine that hides itself primarily in the bland normalcy of an average-looking police officer—required a unique presence. "He had to appear to be an average

kind of guy," said Austin, "and yet there had to be something there to suggest that he wasn't quite one of us. It was difficult finding someone who had that combination of characteristics. But the minute we met Robert Patrick we thought, 'That's the guy.' It was kind of funny because he was the nicest guy in the world, and here he was playing this *mean* character."

Ironically, after months of searching drama schools throughout the country, the part of John Connor went to Edward Furlong, a twelve-year-old Los Angeles resident with virtually no acting experience. "Eddie was totally inexperienced, but he had a wonderful quality that we had not found in anybody else," Austin noted. "And because he had no acting experience, there was a certain honesty about him. He hadn't learned a lot of tricks. From the first time he was on tape, we could

The Terminator and John find a disturbing message that Sarah has carved into a tabletop at the desert compound. The desert location was the first of many employed during the six-month-long production shoot.

tell that he was not at all self-conscious in front of the camera—he was very natural." Once shooting commenced, the filmmakers had to schedule Furlong's work day carefully. Child labor laws mandated a maximum nine-and-a-half-hour day, broken down into four hours of work, three hours of school, an hour of recreation and a half-hour for lunch.

For secondary characters such as truckers and bikers, Cameron opted, whenever possible, to populate his film with authentic types rather than stock Hollywood extras. "We went to amazing lengths to get people who had never been seen before," Austin recalled. "I enlisted the help of a friend of mine who has stayed in touch with a lot of bikers. I offered to buy a drink for anyone who would show up at this bar in Venice. The casting director went and sat with them for two hours, shooting Polaroids to take back and show to Jim. Jim

isn't afraid to take those kinds of risks in casting and he really likes using real people."

While the casting process continued, the producers—along with production designer Joe Nemec—began scouting the numerous locations called for in the script. Because the canal chase was among the first sequences to be shot, scouring over two hundred miles of flood control channel in the Los Angeles area became a priority assignment. "We had two location managers that did the preliminary scouting," said Austin. "They videotaped miles and miles of canal locations, and then we would take a look at it. We weren't concerned too much with aesthetic considerations—a canal is a canal—but there were very particular requirements because of the demands of the script. There had to be an entrance for John to come in on his dirtbike; there had to be another place where he could exit; there had to be a position near the canal where the Terminator could spot John and the tow truck chasing him. We also had to be sure that the clearance heights of all the overpasses were high enough for the tow truck and our production vehicles to pass under. Most importantly, we had to find an intersection above a canal that could be closed and that would enable us to crash the tow truck through a bridge wall and into the canal."

Just as problematic was securing a building to act as the Cyberdyne headquarters. Because shooting in the building was to involve large-scale explosions and vehicles crashing into the lobby, owners of prospective facilities proved somewhat hesitant to welcome the filmmakers. Industrial parks in Los Angeles, San Diego and Camarillo were scouted before a suitable building was located just outside San Jose.

Also needed was an expanse of freeway that could be shut down for two weeks for night shooting of the sequence in which the T-1000, in a helicopter, chases the SWAT van carrying Sarah, John and the Terminator down a busy freeway. After approaching the California

Stunt and effects crew members rig a motorcycle—ridden by Schwarzenegger double Peter Kent—for a spectacular jump into the flood control channel.

A stuntman—doubling for Schwarzenegger—clings to the door of the tanker truck as it careens past the steel mill.

Film Commission, the production secured a two-and-a-half-mile stretch of the Terminal Island Freeway, near Long Beach, which was the only section of urban freeway in southern California that could be effectively closed down all night without creating serious traffic congestion.

By far the most crucial location was the steel mill setting for the final battle in the film. Hoping to find an abandoned but still somewhat functional facility in California, the producers knew of only one option—a massive abandoned steel mill in Fontana. Negotiations with the owners for permission to shoot in the plant were nearly finalized when an independent deal with a Chinese consortium to purchase and relocate the facility threatened to make the site unavailable. "There was extraordinary anxiety for a while there," Austin recalled, "and we started scouting every steel mill in the United States—functioning and nonfunctioning. There was no backup ending for the film—we either had to find a steel mill or build one. Luckily, when the Chinese deal came together, the new owners still allowed us to shoot at the site."

In a whirlwind three months of intense organization and effort, the production team managed to pull together all of the preproduction elements of the film. Effects were designed and already being tested; locations were locked in; budgets were negotiated and approved. Incredibly, in only a little over ninety days, everything had been readied for the start of principal photography.

Cinematographer Adam Greenberg began his career shooting films in his homeland of Israel, so the desert location near Palmdale, California selected for the opening week of principal photography was not at all daunting

Director of photography Adam Greenberg was also cinematographer on the first Terminator *film.*

Coproducers B.J. Rack and Stephanie Austin at the desert compound location.

for him. Nor was the prospect of shooting a high-impact action film. Although most recently his talents had been utilized on gentler fare—such as *Three Men and a Baby* and *Ghost*—he was no stranger to the action genre. He had, in fact, photographed the original *Terminator* and was more than eager to tackle its sequel. "When Jim Cameron called me, I took the job right away," said Greenberg. "I knew the material and I knew the style, and I didn't want anyone else doing *Terminator 2*. I felt like I belonged to it. I knew it would be a tough movie—a very tough movie—but I was happy to be involved."

After several preparatory meetings with Cameron, the truth of Greenberg's assumption became evident. *Terminator 2* was to be a much bigger film than the original—in every way. "On *The Terminator*, I had very little—crewwise and moneywise. This was a big operation, though. Just the scope of it was huge. I had never worked with so many people before. Even Jim was bigger than he'd been on the first film—stronger personality, more sure of what he wanted."

Appropriately, Greenberg approached the filming of this "bigger" film in a bigger way, lighting it with contrasting cold and warm colors and shooting in widescreen Super 35 format. "I went for stronger colors on this film than I did on the first one. The lighting was quite stylistic. On the one hand it is very cold on things like the freeway and the Cyberdyne building where I used many blues and cyan colors. On the other hand, there were contrasting warm colors—very bold. The steel mill, for example, had a lot of cold blues and warm oranges—very strong colors and a lot of contrast."

Rarely was a scene shot with only one camera—even dialogue scenes. Sometimes a half dozen or more were in place. "Multiple cameras are customary on action films," explained Greenberg. "The more cameras, the better. Sometimes you think you have covered something at the right angle and with the right lens, but then you find that the camera with the different lens and at a different angle is better. In an action movie, there are always surprises."

"We were criticized for having the biggest lighting and camera package in history," B.J. Rack elaborated. "But Jim *used* it. When we were out on location in the desert for the scenes in Salceda's camp, we had lines of trucks and four solid camera teams—eight cameras and a Steadicam. And there was some concern about us taking all of that equipment out there. But when it came to the scene where Sarah is cleaning her guns and she looks out and sees John and the Terminator working on the Bronco, talking, Jim was able to set that up and shoot it simultaneously. Although dramatically it is happening at the same time, normally you would never shoot it that way. But he did, using multiple cameras. He called 'action' and the two scenes—with two completely different lighting setups—were shot at the same time."

Most of the effects and action sequences were positioned early in the shooting schedule, not only to avoid outdoor location shooting in the sometimes rainy winter months, but also to ensure that the necessary footage to produce time-consuming visual effects would be completed as quickly as possible. "Computer-generated effects, in particular, take a very long time to perfect," explained Austin, "and these effects were things that nobody had ever done before. So the schedule was front-loaded so that we could supply the footage that ILM needed. Their work necessitated a very long lead time to meet our release date."

After several weeks of daylight shooting in the desert location and the flood control channels, the production moved to San Jose and the Cyberdyne building. Shot entirely at night, the Cyberdyne exteriors required massive lighting setups. "It was very big," said Greenberg. "What we were shooting was actually a boring office building, so I tried to make something more of it with the lighting, making it look almost like a prison with searchlights and spotlights above it. I like shooting at night because I can start from scratch. I don't have to worry about whether the sun will be out or if there will be clouds. I can just start from nothing and do exactly what I want."

In San Jose, as in the desert, the massive equipment inventory proved to be fortuitous.

Astride a motorcycle, the T-1000 bursts through a second-story window of the Cyberdyne building. A stunt rider was harnessed and pulled to safety as the cycle continued on to impact.

"The whole helicopter sequence at Cyberdyne had been intended to be shot in front of a rear projection screen," explained Rack. "But when we got out on location it occurred to us that we could take the mockup helicopter that we had, hang it from a crane, build a little platform under it and shoot it right there. We were there anyway and we had four camera teams. And we got great footage of the burning building behind us—much better than what we probably could have achieved with rear projection."

After a little more than a week in San Jose, night shooting continued for two weeks on the Terminal Island Freeway. The location presented Greenberg with one of the biggest challenges of the show. "I have never before done such a thing as light two-and-a-half miles of freeway. It was very difficult and it took a lot of planning, a lot of thinking ahead. I went to the freeway with my gaffer many

times, beforehand, so that we could map everything out. There was no time for mistakes once we were out there to shoot. We used all of the electric cables existing in Hollywood, I think—we rented them from Fox, Paramount, Universal, Disney. We had eleven generators spread all around, and one-hundred-twenty-foot cranes with lights on them positioned over the full two-and-a-half miles. We used big stadium-type lights and we hung others on existing posts and on a bridge that was there. We had a rigging crew of sixteen people working for eleven days just to set everything up. It was a massive area to cover—the biggest job of the movie."

Once the freeway shoot was completed, cast and crew spent the subsequent weeks between Thanksgiving and the Christmas hiatus at the steel mill in Fontana. In addition to the inherent challenges of lighting and shooting in the dank confines of the old mill,

Greenberg was required to create—with lighting only—the look of molten steel in giant ladles and on the floor. Unfortunately, the production was running late and there was no time allotted to test the ambient lighting setup in conjunction with the internally illuminated steel pours. So when it came time to shoot the molten steel effect, Greenberg had worked out the lighting balance on the basis of theory only. "None of us had had any experience producing this kind of thing before," Greenberg admitted. "But we set it up the best we could. Then on the day we were to shoot, we came in, turned it on—and it didn't look good. It was not 'hot' enough. I felt terrible and could barely look Jim in the face. So we shot around it on that day, and the next day we

went in very early to rearrange everything and put in different gels until the lighting looked right."

After the holidays, work was finished up at the steel mill and the production moved on to the refurbished Lake View Medical Center for a full month of complex action and effects shooting in the psychiatric hospital. Still ahead were the future war sequence back in Fontana, a major shootout in a Santa Monica shopping mall and several weeks of stage work for the Cyberdyne interiors.

For the producers, the hundred-and-some-odd-day shooting schedule was a hectic exercise in making the most out of every minute. "There were always opportunities to set something up while Jim was doing something

The T-1000 skewers Sarah with a metallic finger extension. Cameron sets up the steel mill shot with Linda Hamilton and Robert Patrick.

Schwarzenegger, Cameron and the company prepare for a shot in which Sarah's buried cache of weapons is unearthed.

else," said Rack. "Any down time between setups, we would just get another camera team running. I think we were as organized as any movie has ever been. But even with that, problems came up on the set every day, all the time. And dealing with those problems was our job—putting out fires, day to day."

When principal photography wrapped in late March, only fourteen weeks remained until the scheduled release date. Because of the time required to produce the thousand-plus theatrical prints, however, postproduction had to be completed in an even tighter ten weeks. "It was very tough," Austin com-

mented. "We had only ten weeks in which to mix the soundtrack and music, as well as finish editing the film." The postproduction sound was produced at Skywalker Sound—George Lucas's facility in Marin County. "We picked them because they could do simultaneous effects sound and dialogue," said Rack. "That enabled us to collapse the postproduction schedule by about three weeks—three critical weeks."

To avoid a postproduction editing crunch, Cameron had worked weekends throughout the shooting schedule with editors Conrad Buff and Mark Goldblatt, cutting the film as sequences were photographed. Buff—who had worked successfully with Cameron on *The Abyss*—had been on the project since well before the start of principal photography. "I enjoy working with Jim because he is very strong visually—I really agree with his aesthetic choices. And working in a scope format was enjoyable, too. It's a shape I've always liked and there aren't that many widescreen films being made. So it was a fun project for me to work on." Goldblatt—who had edited the original *Terminator*—joined the team midway through principal photography.

Both editors concentrated their earliest efforts on cutting together the long chase sequences—notably, the dirtbike canal chase and the helicopter freeway chase. "In the chase sequences," said Buff, "we had to make a lot of quick cuts—and building that kind of structure takes a long time. We were always looking for interesting pieces; and because the duration of each piece was so short, it took many days to build up a sequence. Jim has a very frantic approach to action sequences, as opposed to some directors who block them out so perfectly that they go together mechanically. Jim does a lot of homework and knows exactly what he is after; but to arrive at that, he shoots the material in a slightly uncontrolled way. What you get from that is a lot more exciting—and a lot more fun to work on."

Though the editors were given a great deal of leeway in structuring the chase sequences as they saw fit, Cameron's weekly input was invaluable. "More than anyone I've ever worked with, Jim knows what he has on film. He remembers all the nuances and details of damn near every take. He is a stickler for details and there are things that are peculiar to him that he likes to see—either in a charac-ter or in visual terms—that might go by me, but make a difference in the film ultimately. In the canal chase, for example, Arnold is riding through a series of gates along the top of the canal, shooting the locks off of the gates as he goes. To keep the energy and pace going, I had him shoot one lock off and then cross the street and shoot again. And Jim looked at that and said, 'No, no—he has to cock the gun first.' He knows his machinery and hardware and he wants them presented accurately."

Buff also found Cameron's use of multiple cameras to be an interesting challenge. "He choreographs things wonderfully and is able to use multiple camera setups in a unique way. A lot of directors are very traditional about it—there is the master A camera and the B camera is on something else. A lot of Jim's material doesn't have a traditional master. In *Terminator 2* there were a lot of physical stunts and gags that required multiple camera setups. He'd have six or seven cameras going, and staging those scenes . . . I'm not quite sure how he did it."

From editors to the director of photography to the producers, the consensus seemed to be, "We're not quite sure how he did it." "I don't know how we could have made all of this work with a different director," noted Rack. "You hear that Jim is difficult, but from our point of view he was *easy*. He was able to think through, logistically, really massive problems with massive ramifications. And because he was able to visualize everything so completely, we were able to break down every sequence of the film in great detail. Considering how difficult a project it was, and how short a schedule we had, it was really incredible how it all came together."

5 December 1990, Fontana, California

On this windy night, the production is shooting in a cavernous steel mill that has been abandoned for seventeen years—and looks it. The final showdown between the time-displaced titans will take place here. Two hundred feet tall from floor to ceiling and a thousand feet in length, the barnlike building is not the most pleasant place in which to work. Seventeen years' worth of dirt is everywhere, kicked up by the wind which is funneled and accelerated as it blows through the open door at one end. Rows of boxcar-size cargo containers have been stacked outside to act as windbreakers, but still the wind and dust blow hard enough that many of the crew members wear surgical masks over their faces.

There is evidence here and there of production designer Joe Nemec's five-week stint at the steel mill prior to the company's arrival, although most of the add-on work blends seamlessly into the surroundings. Near the open doorway, a gigantic ladle is suspended in a tilting position. A long coral-colored piece of Fiberglas extends from its spout to a large receptacle beneath it. When lit from within and bathed with flowing methylcellulose slime, it will look very much like white-hot molten steel.

In the broad entryway to the building, a liquid nitrogen truck lies jackknifed on its side. Twenty yards ahead of it, a small pickup has been rammed into a large forklift. One of the forklift teeth has skewered the truck cab through front and rear windshields. Two stunt performers had done the gag live the night before. Amid such chaos, all four of the principal characters have found their way into the mill.

Inside the pickup sit Eddie Furlong and Linda Hamilton. Hamilton is a petite woman—not much bigger than her twelve-year-old costar. Even so, she looks tough in army boots and black combat gear, her bare arms sporting well-defined muscles and a cigarette in her

mouth. Schwarzenegger double Peter Kent is in makeup and costume and standing a few feet from the truck. Cameron leans on the door, instructing the two actors inside. He is about to shoot their retreat from the truck immediately following its crash into the forklift. They rehearse the scene a couple of times for the camera while Cameron watches the action on a video monitor. Shaken and injured by the collision, Sarah and John watch through the shattered rear windshield as the Terminator fires a handgun—supposedly at the unstoppable T-1000 who has emerged off-camera from the overturned liquid nitrogen truck. Sarah and John stumble out of the cab to make their escape. Sarah is limping and there is blood on her leg. John holds her up and together they run deeper into the confines of the steel mill.

It is now time to shoot. Two makeup people spray glistening water on Furlong's face and Hamilton's hair, which is already in serious disarray. Fake blood is applied to her leg and smeared a bit on her arms. The makeup people work quickly, efficiently, and then get out of the way.

Assistant director Mike Haynie calls "Sparks, please!" and crew members in the rafters start up a shower of sparks that rain down on the scene. Cameron calls "Action!" Four men squatted at the base of the pickup begin rocking it violently back and forth to simulate its movement immediately after the crash. Hamilton and Furlong stare in horror out the back of the truck as the Terminator kneels and fires at their adversary. Two cameras record the action: one is a closeup of Hamilton, the other a longer shot of the two of them.

As the truck rocks and the sparks fly, the director talks his actors through the scene: "Come on out, Eddie . . . that's it. Terminator rises . . . and *boom!*" The action is complete and Cameron calls "Cut." The sparks stop. The actors relax. The crew is already busy preparing for the next setup. There is no time to waste.

Hamilton is having Polaroid snapshots taken from all angles for continuity purposes. Furlong talks to crew members, looking tired. A producer offers him her chair, which he plops down into. Within seconds, though, he is up and off.

The real Arnold Schwarzenegger is needed for the next shot. When he arrives from the makeup trailer, the right side of his face shows signs of the gunshot wounds and other abuse the Terminator has suffered to date in the film. Parts of the cyborg endoskeleton can be seen on his forehead, chest and knees. Smoking a cigar that looks huge, even in his hands, Schwarzenegger jokes with the crew and converses with Peter Kent about the upcoming shot—Kent has already been through the actions three or four times. Schwarzenegger is a good three inches shorter than his double.

The shot is rehearsed. With the cigar still clenched incongruously between his teeth, the Terminator fires at the off-camera T-1000. John runs to him, tugging on his arm; then he returns to Sarah, helping her out of the pickup. The Terminator limps to the bed of the truck and unhurriedly grabs a grenade launcher before joining his fleeing companions.

After rehearsal, while the shot is readied, Hamilton watches the takes of her previous scene on video playback. She seems pleased. Then she wanders over to talk with her stunt double and another woman about the travails of nighttime shooting. No one is accustomed to the schedule yet. Cameron walks by. Hamilton gives him a tired hug, her head just barely reaching his chest. There is still a very long night ahead.

The Terminator at the steel mill. The final stage makeup—revealing sections of the cyborg's chrome endoskeleton—was created and executed by Stan Winston and his crew.

COMING TOGETHER AGAIN

T2 One thing was clear to Jim Cameron long before *Terminator 2* emerged as a viable project—any plans for a sequel to his 1984 hit would have to include Arnold Schwarzenegger and Linda Hamilton. Although Schwarzenegger had starred in a succession of other action films and had even ventured creditably into light comedy since the first film was released, the actor remained so identified with *The Terminator* that a sequel without him in the title role would have been unthinkable. Hamilton, too, was crucial to the project since, in Cameron's mind, the logical continuation of the first story would have to revolve dramatically around the character of Sarah Connor. As much as he wanted *Terminator 2* to become a reality, Cameron was prepared to dismiss the project entirely if either Hamilton or Schwarzenegger was unwilling or unable to participate.

Fortunately, both actors were enthusiastic about the prospect of doing a sequel. Schwarzenegger had, in fact, first broached the subject before *The Terminator* was released, and Hamilton had discussed the possibility with Cameron several times throughout the years. When the project finally came together, both Hamilton and Schwarzenegger—in a remarkable leap of faith—signed on without even having read a completed script.

Though it was seven years from the release of the first film before the cast was reunited for the sequel, Hamilton, whose star had risen through the success of her *Beauty and the Beast* television series, had never doubted that the film would be made. "My instincts told me that there would be a *Terminator 2* someday, even though it took a long time. Jim credited much of the success of *Aliens* to the fact that it had been done so many years after the first film, so I knew he didn't consider that to be an obstacle. There was no time restriction in bringing the film together; and when it finally happened, I wasn't surprised."

Hamilton, for one, was glad that *Terminator 2* was so long in coming to fruition since it gave her the opportunity to mature both as a person and as an actress. "I have a whole wealth of experience that I was able to bring to this film. I was a much newer actress when I did *The Terminator*, which was all right because that Sarah Connor was younger and more frail. But there is a lot that has happened to me since then and all of that experience made a great contribution to the character. I feel more like Sarah now than I did in the first film. Like her, I have a son that I am raising alone. So, personally, the film is very significant to me at this time in my life. And it is a film against nuclear war, which is certainly timely."

Cameron confers with actors Linda Hamilton,
Joe Morton and Arnold Schwarzenegger
in preparation for the destruction of Cyberdyne.

From her earliest discussions with Cameron, Hamilton had realized that the Sarah of *Terminator 2* was to be a very different character from the one she had created in the original film. "That was great because, as an actress, I wasn't really interested in playing that character again—I'd already done it. This was to be a much greater challenge; as hard as it gets, I think. There was so much I had to bring up for this role: the fear of annihilation, the anger, the bitterness. Jim told me early on that he was going to make her crazy, and I said, 'Yeah. The crazier, the better.' It was tough because I knew the audience wouldn't necessarily like me very much, but that was part of the challenge."

Hamilton was also intrigued by the way in which *Terminator 2* brought the character of Sarah full circle from the naive girl of the first story to the hardened warrior of the second. "There was a wonderful Everywoman quality about Sarah in *The Terminator*. She was a normal girl who changed and grew strong through the course of the film. But in *Terminator 2*, she has set aside all the basic principles of humanity and there is no love in her life. She is like John the Baptist—a voice crying out in the wilderness. She's wild and lost, broken and angry, with nothing but ashes inside. And then, eventually, she is rehumanized. So this role is transformational in the opposite way. She goes from being someone who is cold and hard to someone who rediscovers her humanity."

The sequel reveals a Sarah who has undergone a physical transformation as well. In preparation for the horrific war to come, Sarah has become well-schooled in the use of weapons and combat techniques. She's now a lean, strong, muscled soldier. For almost four months prior to the start of filming, Hamilton subjected herself to rigorous training. "As

Sarah Connor takes cover during a battle with a SWAT team in the Cyberdyne building.

Linda Hamilton prepared for her return as Sarah Connor with weeks of intensive military-type training.

soon as I read the script I realized that I would have to commit myself to really getting in shape. I began working with a personal trainer six mornings a week, two to three hours a day. I lifted weights and did a lot of aerobic conditioning. It was wonderful to see myself transformed. I had muscles and I was a hundred times stronger than I had ever been, which was a good thing because I would never have made it through the film otherwise. I was battered and chased and slammed into walls and everything else. Every day was a physical challenge; but because of the training, I was prepared for it. I was as much of an Arnold Schwarzenegger as I could be."

Hamilton also underwent military-style training with commando trainer Uzi Gal, learning how to handle weapons and hand-to-hand combat techniques. "I did that for two months, and they were the longest two months of my life. It was grueling. I could

have stopped at any time, but I didn't because I knew that this was the process Sarah had gone through. It had beaten her down and made her old and wise and strong and I had to understand all of that before I could do the role. So even though it was very, very hard, the training helped me to focus on Sarah and understand her. She doesn't have room in her life for an expression or a smile. She's all business, because in this kind of combat there is no place for emotion. If your weapon jams, you don't get mad, you fix it—or you die."

It was that 'all business,' cigarette-smoking, gun-packing woman in army fatigues and boots that Hamilton portrayed throughout most of the film. However, a sequence in which Kyle Reese appears to Sarah in a dream afforded the actress the opportunity to show Sarah at her most vulnerable. "It was very important because it was the only scene in which the love story from the first film was

recaptured. It had to be powerful and passionate. Her love for this man is the thing that has fueled Sarah Connor all of these years, and we had to show that. We shot it in the middle of the shooting schedule, after we'd already done a lot of the action stuff. I had been beaten up and I was tired; so there was a tremendous emotional release in doing the scene. And it was the day the war started in the Middle East. So my heart hurt. I couldn't stop crying at the end of the day."

The dream sequence was the only scene in which Michael Biehn, Hamilton's *Terminator* costar, appeared. Biehn had worked with Cameron not only in *The Terminator* but also in *Aliens* and *The Abyss*, and it was during the filming of the latter film that the actor and director discussed the possibility of bringing back the character of Kyle Reese for *Terminator 2*. "We thought about it and tossed ideas around," said Biehn, "but neither one of us could come up with a way to bring the character back. So I knew early on that I wouldn't be too involved in the sequel. Later, Jim mentioned that he was thinking of writing a kind of flashback scene and I told him I'd love to do that, especially if it had something to do with the love story. I thought the nicest thing about the role was Reese's relationship with Sarah."

Ultimately, the short scene between Reese and Sarah required Biehn's presence on the set for only one day. Prior to filming, however, the actor had spent numerous hours in rehearsal with Cameron and Hamilton. "We got together a couple of nights, just to talk about it and work out the scene. Jim is very open to ideas from actors, which is a great situation to be in. It is a short scene that took only a couple of hours to shoot, but we put in quite a bit of time discussing it and getting it right."

Although his role in *Terminator 2* amounted to little more than a cameo appearance, Biehn was more than happy to collaborate once again with both Hamilton and Cameron. "I owe much of my career to Jim. If he asked me to mow his lawn, I'd do it. And I have had a very good relationship with Linda since the first film. I'm proud of our scene in *Terminator 2* and I was pleased to be a part of the film, even in a small way. I don't think people will walk away from the theater saying, 'Whatever happened to old Reese?' Because the scene was such an important one, I think the audience will feel that Reese was there."

Biehn's involvement in the film helped to make *Terminator 2* something of a homecoming for Linda Hamilton. "It was very satisfying to work with Michael and Arnold and Jim again. I have always had great affection for Michael and working with Arnold was a hoot—he is larger than life and a very funny man. And I have come to respect Jim Cameron enormously. I don't think I realized what a talented director he was when I was doing *The Terminator*. I thought he was doing just another action picture. But then I saw the film and realized he had something much more interesting in mind. Working with Jim on *Terminator 2* was almost like a romance; I felt very well partnered. He made me feel nurtured and appreciated and, unlike the first film, working with him was a collaboration. So, for me, *Terminator 2* was a complete experience. I even got to work with my twin sister and my baby. In the steel mill, when the T-1000 transforms into Sarah, I played the T-1000 and my sister played Sarah. She got to shoot me in the back. And in the playground scene during Sarah's dream of a nuclear attack, I got to hold my own son. The whole film was a wonderful coming together again."

For Arnold Schwarzenegger, it was a sense of inevitability fulfilled when *Terminator 2* finally muscled its way onto the production docket of Carolco Pictures seven years after its predecessor had redefined the standards for science fiction adventure movies. It was a dream that he had continued to nurture even when others essential to the project became disenchanted by the tangled web of proprietary interests that seemed terminally at odds.

"Certain films lend themselves to sequels and others do not," Schwarzenegger observed. "If you have one that does not and you try to force it, it will usually fall on its face—which happens too often with sequels. But with *Terminator*, even before the film came out, Jim and I realized that this could be an ongoing character in an ongoing story. We talked about it then, and we also kind of made a commitment that neither one of us would make it

Sarah and Reese are reunited in a dream sequence. The short but poignant scene was the only one in which Terminator *alumnus Michael Biehn appeared.*

Arnold Schwarzenegger relaxes between takes at the desert location. Though a veteran of many successful action films and comedies, the Terminator had remained one of the actor's favorite roles.

as long as Hemdale was involved it would never happen," stated Schwarzenegger, "because Hemdale was not a company that was capable of making a classy movie that demanded a big budget—they would want to make it cheap. That we knew for sure. So no one would make a deal with them. I wouldn't after the first experience, nor would Jim Cameron. We knew we should forget about a sequel if Hemdale kept the rights." Years later, however, after a string of blockbuster hits, Schwarzenegger found that his name and enthusiasm, coupled with the assured participation of James Cameron, was more than enough to persuade the high-profile Carolco Pictures to buy out Hemdale's interest in *The Terminator* and set the sequel in motion.

Had the impetus for involving Schwarzenegger in the initial film been acted upon, the cinematic superstar would not have been a player in the sequel. Schwarzenegger was first approached regarding the project by Mike Medavoy, then executive vice president of Orion Pictures, distributor of the projected Hemdale production. "Mike Medavoy came up to me during a screening of *Blue Thunder*, and he said, 'Look, there's this movie we're doing that has a great part in it. We have O.J. Simpson for the Terminator and we'd like you to play Reese.' So I got in touch with Jim Cameron and read the script. During our second meeting, I began talking about the Terminator character and how he had to be like a machine and how he had to walk and how he had to act and how he had to have no emotion. And whoever played him had to be thoroughly trained in weapons so that he could load and cock the guns without ever having to look down at the ammunition or the magazine. We also talked a little bit about Reese. Later, Jim called my agent and said: 'I want Arnold to play the Terminator. He understands the character.' And I realized that he was right. I was a lot more enthusiastic about the Terminator than I was about Reese. Everyone around me said, 'Maybe you shouldn't play a villain. It might be bad for your career.' I thought about it for a little bit; but by then I was hooked on playing the Terminator."

Though Schwarzenegger had gravitated, almost unconsciously, to the Terminator part in

without the other one. We realized how many negative forces were involved at that point, and we wanted to make sure that no one would try to split us up or do their own little trip."

Among the players that Schwarzenegger considered to be 'negative forces' was Hemdale Film Corporation, the independent production company that had backed the first *Terminator*. Committed to modest budgets and tight control, Hemdale, it was thought, lacked the vision or the resources to proceed with a sequel that would be many times more ambitious than the original. "I realized that

the first film, his most memorable role would be somewhat reversed in the second. No longer the implacable killer sent through time to destroy the future of mankind, he was now its potential savior pitted against another terminator even more advanced than himself. Schwarzenegger found the role reversal intriguing, though he draws the line at redefining his character as a 'good guy.' "I would not consider the Terminator to be a good guy, believe me. He has been programmed to protect the kid; but aside from that, nothing much is changed. Ask any of the other people he destroys in the film. I am playing—in comparison to the first Terminator—a somewhat more comfortable fellow, but that's about it."

Over the years, Schwarzenegger had fostered visions of himself portraying both terminators in the sequel, an idea put forth to him by Jim Cameron shortly after the release of the original film. The notion eventually went by the wayside, though, and Schwarzenegger did not resist. "When we went to Cannes last year, Jim told me that he had changed that approach—that he did not want the bottom line of the story to be that I was playing two characters. And I totally understood that. Jim is someone I respect to the highest. When you trust someone and trust their talent, it's not necessary to question things as much. If Jim was comfortable with the decision, then so was I. Working with Jim Cameron is quite unique because he's basically *everything*! He writes the script, he comes up with the concept, he directs you on your scenes. He wants to do his own lighting and he wants to do his own filming. He wants to do everything. You see him running with the smoke machine and you see him putting on blood and trying to do your makeup even though the makeup and special effects departments have already done the job. But he has to improve on it somehow. So he really has his fingers in every aspect of the film. He has a very clear vision and a Jim Cameron movie has a distinctive look because it's a total rep-

Reprogrammed, the Terminator marshalls his deadly skills to protect young John Connor. Schwarzenegger was intrigued at the prospect of portraying a sympathetic Terminator.

resentation of what *he* wants to see. That vision is one of the reasons I enjoyed working with Jim again."

While *Terminator 2* was a reunion of sorts for Hamilton and Schwarzenegger, actors Robert Patrick and Edward Furlong, playing, respectively, the new characters of the T-1000 and ten-year-old John Connor, found themselves stepping into somewhat daunting and unfamiliar territory. Having worked primarily playing villains in low-budget Roger Corman productions—coincidentally, the same arena in which Cameron began his filmmaking career—Patrick suddenly found himself in the big leagues, working with a name director and two major stars in a motion picture that seemed destined to be a blockbuster. It was undeniably heady stuff for a young actor who only a few years earlier had driven from his home in Cleveland to Hollywood in hopes of launching a film career.

A fan of the original *Terminator*, Patrick first met with casting director Mali Finn to do a video screentest that was subsequently reviewed by Jim Cameron. Because of the secrecy of the project, Patrick was given vague instructions during the test, but remained uncertain as to the exact nature of the character. "All my agent had told me was to be the most intense, fearsome, scariest guy I could be," Patrick recalled. "Then when I got together with Mali for the video, she gave me a feeling for the character without giving away who or what he was."

Impressed with the initial video improvisation, Cameron called Patrick back the next day to meet with him and work in video once again, this time under the direction of Cameron himself. "Jim and I hit it off well. I could see right away that he was a cool guy; and because I knew he'd worked with Roger early in his career, I felt comfortable with him. Jim showed me the storyboards and told me a little more about the character and I began to realize that this was a great role. Inside I was thinking, 'I can do this—I've *got* to get this!' "

After more auditions and meetings with Cameron, Patrick finally landed the role of the T-1000 and immediately began training with Steve Cook, a personal friend and a martial arts master. "I did this on my own, as

Robert Patrick as the T-1000's human form. Before winning the role, Patrick had worked primarily playing villains in low-budget movies.

character development. I learned how to control my body, how to stretch it out to make it look fluid. I even changed my breathing. Steve suggested that I go through all of my workouts breathing through my nose. I found that breathing through the nose evenly—even while running very fast—helped to create a machinelike quality in the T-1000."

Patrick also prepared for his role by training with Uzi Gal. "I wasn't forced to do it—I had already been in pretty good shape when I auditioned for the role—but it was a great opportunity because I knew I'd get something out of it that I could use. So I went from a period of

On a search-and-destroy mission, the T-1000 prowls the corridors of the mental hospital where Sarah Connor is incarcerated.

learning to relax and stretch and let my muscles go with the martial arts to an intense period of working on my body in a completely different way. We did weightlifting, strengthening my legs so that I'd be able to sprint very fast and run without fatigue after a lot of takes. It was very military and very tough. The first day I worked out with Uzi I didn't know if I was going to get through it. We worked from about five o'clock in the morning, three or four workouts a day, every day for nine weeks. It actually changed my lifestyle some. I quit smoking, for one thing. It also helped me to grow as a person and to focus on the character. When you go into a role like this, you've got to go full throttle."

By the time shooting started in October, Patrick was in peak form, both physically and mentally prepared to take on the difficult role. The primary challenge for Patrick was creating a compelling character who spoke very little dialogue and was virtually emotionless. "Because there wasn't a lot of dialogue, I had to rely on physical presence and come up with things to make him interesting. I used my eyes to create a kind of intensity, as if there was a lot going on inside of him. One of the things I did with my eyes was to hold them on the target, never blinking. I would lock onto a target, as if there was straight line between us, and then my body would just carry me there, smoothly and without effort. The T-1000 had to be fluid, effortless, almost as if he could float. He was centered when he walked, everything coming from the gut, balanced, which is the basis of the martial arts. I also adopted a military posture to give him a powerful look. Then, when he was supposed to be a human— interacting as the cop with other characters— I would relax into a more casual stance. The whole thing was very subtle, so subtle that every once in a while I would worry that I wasn't putting out enough. I'd think, 'Ooh, if I could only play this like a human, he'd be *raging*!' But I could only have the rage inside. On the outside I had to remain cool."

As the T-1000, Patrick was called upon to do hand-to-hand battle with Arnold Schwarzenegger, a challenging prospect for the slight-statured actor still somewhat in awe of the Schwarzenegger image. "I was scared about matching up to him physically. The first time I met him, it was like, 'Wow . . . that's *Arnold Schwarzenegger*!' I had to psych myself up for fighting him by telling myself that my character was more advanced than he was and that I could hold my own with him. He was bigger than me and a hell of a lot stronger, but I had learned from the martial arts training that a little guy can take on a big guy. When we got to the fight scenes, I was mentally prepared and it was great! I would slam him against something and then, when it was done, back away and kind of snicker to myself, 'Jesus Christ, I'm beatin' up Arnold!' But there was one point where he had to grab me and I really felt the power of Arnold Schwarzenegger. My toes were off the floor and he was dragging me back and forth—bam! bam! bam! bam! And I was thinking, 'Shit! He's got me in the air!' But when it was my turn to get the better of him, he helped a lot. He just went with it and he was great."

Unlike the adversarial role played by Robert Patrick, thirteen-year-old Edward Furlong's assignment was the role of John Connor, Sarah's ten-year-old son who, through the course of the film, forms a bond of friendship with the Terminator. The young resident of Pasadena had had no previous acting experience when Mali Finn literally picked him out of a crowd of boys at the local boys club to read for the role. "She was there looking for kids that looked like Linda Hamilton and Michael Biehn," said Furlong, "and she just found me. The funny thing about it was that I didn't even want to go to the boys club that day but my uncle, who I live with, made me go. I was talking to some friends and Mali came up and said, 'Would you be interested in trying out for this part?' She took a Polaroid of me and I went home and told my aunt and uncle and they thought, 'Oh, sure. It's probably some weirdo or someone doing an X-rated movie.' But then Mali called my aunt and told her it was *Terminator 2*, and my aunt knew that it was going to be a real big movie."

Furlong's first audition was a loose videotaped session with Mali Finn. When Cameron saw the tape, he set up a second audition in which Furlong read with Linda Hamilton. "That audition didn't go so great," recalled

Edward Furlong as the street-smart John Connor. Furlong was spotted at a local boys club by casting director Mali Finn.

John lends aid to his injured mother as they flee through the steel mill.

Furlong, "because I was nervous about working with Linda. After that audition I thought, 'Forget it, I'm not getting this part.' But then they gave me a dialogue coach and after working with him for a while, I auditioned one last time with Jim Cameron and that one was good. Jim said he'd tell me in a couple of days if I got the part, but then he decided to tell me that day. When he told me I got it, I was real calm about it but when I got out to the car it was: 'Ahhh! Yes! Yes! Yes!' I was hitting the top of the car and everything."

Even after winning the part, Furlong had trouble believing his own good fortune. In the weeks before filming began, the neophyte actor feared that he would be replaced by someone else and frequently had dreams of getting to the set only to discover another 'John Connor' there. His fears proved unfounded, however, when he joined the cast and crew in the Lancaster desert location and began a six-month moviemaking stint that was to be far different from the life he had known as a seventh grader in a Pasadena public school.

His typical day on the set was broken up into time spent in makeup, in the school trailer and in front of the camera. "The hardest thing was switching back and forth. I had to switch from thinking about being John Connor to thinking about math or Spanish. But everyone was very nice to me and it was a lot of fun being in a movie. I tried not to get a swollen head about it. Most of my friends didn't really care that I was making a movie. At first I talked about it a lot but then everybody was like, 'Who cares?' So I just talked about what was going on in school and if I'd missed any pretty girls while I was gone; stuff like that."

Cameron had worried that the young actor might crumble under the pressure when shooting actually began; but from the first day on the set, Furlong showed remarkable aplomb. "I wasn't nervous. It was just fun. On the first day we did a scene that was a closeup of me, and Jim was really impressed and happy. Then he found Chapstick on my lips, and in the playback it looked weird and shiny and he was really mad. I was able to repeat what I'd done before, but I felt bad. It was like,

John finds an unlikely friend in the Terminator. Furlong often eased moviemaking tedium by clowning on the set with the affable Schwarzenegger.

'Oh, no—not on my first day!'"

Furlong even managed to stay calm in the face of working with Schwarzenegger, an undisputed hero to literally millions of his teenage peers. "I was really nervous about meeting him at the beginning," Furlong admitted, "but then I got to know him better and he's not so special. I clowned around a lot with Arnold, and then Jim would walk by and get pissed off because he didn't like us clowning around when we were doing a scene. Arnold could just switch it on and off—from the Terminator to Arnold and then back to the Terminator again—but I couldn't do that. So sometimes Arnold would want to clown around and I

wouldn't want to, but it was hard to say no."

Though Furlong's life returned to normal when shooting wrapped in March, the *Terminator 2* experience left an indelible impression on the young man. "I'd love to keep acting, or maybe become a director or producer. At least now I know more about what it's like. I had thought about going into acting before all of this happened, but back then I didn't know what the sacrifices are. It's very hard. You have to go in front of a hundred people and show them how good an actor you are or how bad an actor you are."

Terminator 2 meant different things to different cast members. For Linda Hamilton it was a very personal 'coming together again' with old colleagues and friends. For Arnold Schwarzenegger it was a chance to return to the role that had been the breakthrough to an astonishing career. For Robert Patrick it was a giant leap from 'B' movie obscurity to big-time filmmaking. And for Edward Furlong it was an unexpected and delightful adventure. For all the actors, however, *Terminator 2* was a challenge that demanded an unwavering personal commitment. "I really invested myself in this character and in this movie," concluded Linda Hamilton. "I loved this picture and, more than anything, I wanted to do it proud."

6 December 1990, Fontana, California

A major shot is in the works. A scene is needed of the overturned liquid nitrogen truck sliding to rest in the steel mill doorway. Jim Cameron is up on a platform, part of the existing structure, which overlooks the setup. He has a viewfinder in hand and is working with two extras dressed as steelworkers. They are supposed to react to the scene and then flee past camera. One of them isn't getting the message that his director wants him to move *fast*. Cameron is getting impatient. Once the two have mastered the concept, Cameron calls for makeup to dirty them up and descends to the main floor to specify precise start and stop points for the truck. Cameron is nothing if not specific.

Thomas Fisher and his effects crew work feverishly to prepare the shot. The tractor rig is already on its side and separated from the cylindrical tanker which is likewise tipped over and crushed open. Both need to move only a few feet. A steel cable is attached to the frame of the tractor and run across the floor to a bulldozer sitting off-camera. On cue, the dozer will tug the tractor smartly into its final position. A forklift hidden behind the severed tanker trailer will push the rear half of the rig forward at the same moment. A large dump-tank has been erected out of view and stands ready to spill hundreds of gallons of water out onto the floor. Simultaneously, canisters of liquid nitrogen will release clouds of frigid vapor from the ruptured tanker vessel.

In addition to the platform camera, another is positioned at an even higher vantage point while still another is erected on the ground level. Two small remote cameras are placed on the floor near the anticipated resting place of the tractor. The giant ladle will be in view for the first time and the megawatt lighting system designed to make its contents look like molten steel is fired up. It is bright to the eye, but not brilliant—the camera will provide that effect by selective exposure.

From a prime vantage point nearby, Cameron observes coverage from his main cameras on multiple video monitors. Ten cues must be given for the shot to go as planned. To make sure he forgets none of them, Cameron has written them on a piece of paper and taped them to the video cart in front of him. "Smoke!" Smoke machines start pumping dense atmospheric smoke into the setup. "Sparks!" A shower of sparks is unleased from the rafters. "Nitrogen!"

"Cut! Cut!" A voice rings out. It isn't Cameron's. The first rule of moviemaking flashes through everyone's mind. Nobody but the director calls a cut—ever.

Sound mixer Lee Orloff looks up from his console. "What is it?" says Cameron. Over his headset, Orloff has heard that the principal platform camera is out of commission and it was he who made the call. A moment later and it would have been too late. A faulty battery is reported. Cameron growls at the camera operator for not checking his equipment during the two hours it had taken to set up the shot.

Then he turns to his sound man. "Thanks, Lee."

Visual effects team members from Industrial Light and Magic are on the set. Background material is being shot that will later be combined with computer-generated imagery. The scenes needed are of T-1000 reforming into his humanoid shape after being frozen solid by spilled liquid nitrogen and shattered to pieces by gunfire directed at him by the Terminator. The untended ladle has overflowed its receptacle and molten steel is pouring out onto the floor, melting the frozen shards back into their liquid metal state.

Much activity is afoot, with preparations in progress for a succession of shots. To create the effect of molten steel on the floor, a fifty-square-foot section of flooring has been fashioned from translucent acrylic and backed with high-wattage lamps. Masonite templates are screwed into place overtop to suggest the first phase of the spill. Successive templates will broaden the illuminated area. A barrel filled with Duraflame logs blazes nearby. Prior to the shot, crumbling bits of the fiery material will be shoveled into

Amid showering sparks, molten steel pours from a giant ladle onto the steel mill floor. Backlit acrylic floor panels were used to simulate the spill.

place along the leading edge of the spill.

Across the set, two large cartons are opened by members of the makeup effects crew. Inside, individually wrapped in tissue, are cast strips of rigid urethane with chromed T-1000 shards attached like plastic model kit pieces. Anyone with nothing better to do joins in the task of unwrapping and separating the individual shards. In a while, they will be scattered onto the floor in front of the leaking tanker truck.

Although the principal effects will be generated by computer, for reference purposes and for distant out-of-focus views something is needed on set to represent the fluid T-1000 massing together and swelling up. Cameron suggests pinning sheets of mylar onto a sound blanket and placing it over someone who can crouch down on the floor and then rise up like a chrome blob. Van Ling—Cameron's ever-present right-hand man—is volunteered for the dubious honor.

For similar types of shots, Marlene Stewart's wardrobe department has fashioned a semi-rigid mylar suit representing T-1000 in full humanoid form, yet still in his transitional chrome state. Pasha Afshar—doubling for Robert Patrick—shows up on the set wearing it for Cameron's appraisal. On his face is a gleaming likeness of the actor's fabricated by the Stan Winston unit. The director—who has been on his hands and knees with a wardrobe lady attaching sheets of mylar onto blankets—studies the figure front and back. "The ears stick out too much." No problem, he is assured. Afshar—who can barely see or walk in the chrome straitjacket and mask—toddles off like an unoiled Tin Man to have his ears taped back.

ACTION IN EVERY PARAGRAPH

T2 Stunt coordinator Gary Davis's first response upon reading the *Terminator 2* script was that it would be an easy project—provided the shooting schedule was two years long. It was not, of course. Instead, the production was slated to be shot in less than five months, making it a harrowing prospect even for this sixteen-year veteran of action films. "There was action in every paragraph of the script," Davis recalled. "It was just jam-packed full. I knew it would be an incredible undertaking. It was the biggest picture I had ever done—possibly the biggest picture *anybody* had ever done."

Despite the magnitude of the assignment and the shortness of the schedule, Davis agreed not only to coordinate the film's stunts but also to direct the second unit photography. Working closely with special effects supervisor Thomas Fisher—who would execute the numerous physical gags—Davis assembled a crew of top-notch stunt performers and a second unit crew that included director of photography Michael Benson, who was well qualified to match the cinematic style of the picture, having worked many times before with Adam Greenberg.

Early in the shooting schedule, Davis and Fisher worked hand in hand on the elaborate chase staged within the Los Angeles County flood control channel system. Fleeing from the T-1000, John dirtbikes into the canal—an evasive tactic that fails when the T-1000, driving a massive tow truck, crashes through an overpass wall and successfully makes the fifteen-foot drop to continue his pursuit.

The truck's dive into the canal was an involved setup. "We built a false soft plaster extension on top of the existing retaining wall," explained Fisher, "then topped it with a lightweight aluminum railing so that the truck could crash through it more easily, without sustaining terrible damage. A dummy driver was placed inside the tow truck, which had been gutted of all engine parts to make it as lightweight as possible. The gutted truck was cabled to a tow truck that was at an angle, out of frame, and pulled toward a ramp which we had built up to the top of the retaining wall. At the point of impact, its speed was about forty miles per hour. As the truck hit the ramp and crashed through the plaster wall, we cut the cables and the vehicle flew through the air and dropped into the canal below."

To catch the action up close without endan-

John Connor dirtbikes through a narrow concrete canal, tailed closely by the T-1000 in a tow truck.

gering anyone, four remote cameras were hidden amid the debris in the canal. "We also had three cameras farther down, shooting with long lenses," noted effects liaison Van Ling. "Stuntman Bobby Porter—who was doubling for John—sat halfway between the cameras and the spot where the truck was supposed to come down; but with the long lens, the image was compressed to look like the truck landed right behind him." Incredibly, the heavy-duty truck survived the stunt and it was able to be used for the remainder of the sequence.

As the T-1000 gives chase in the canal, the Terminator follows, making a spectacular motorcycle leap into the canal bottom. Because the fifteen-foot jump was deemed too dangerous to be executed as a stunt, Fisher and his crew rigged the motorcycle onto a cable which was hung from crane arms on either side of the canal. "The cable was pulled tight like a clothesline between the two cranes," explained Fisher. "The motorcycle was attached to the cable and also to a pickup truck that pulled it down into the canal. There was a pulley on each end that would release the cable a little bit at a time as the motorcycle descended. Peter Kent was riding the motorcycle, so we lowered it fairly slowly as a safety precaution." By shooting the action at a low frame rate, the slow descent was

made to look like a free-fall jump on film. The cables were later removed from the shots by Industrial Light and Magic, using a computer graphics program they had developed to perfection.

Between first and second unit photography, nearly five full weeks were spent in the canals to complete the complex chase sequence. By contrast, both units had only a week and a half to execute numerous requirements at the Cyberdyne building—the site of some of the film's most elaborate stunts and special effects.

With a massive explosion inside the building, Sarah, John and the Terminator succeed in destroying the seminal research that would have launched the Skynet project. The blast—photographed from without—was realized by blowing out most of the second-floor windows and simultaneously creating massive fireballs that mushroomed into the sky. "We taped primer cord on the windows which was detonated electronically," explained Fisher. "To create the fireball, we took plastic trash bags, put about five gallons of gasoline in them and set them inside twenty-gallon drums that had black powder charges at the bottom. We made up about twenty of those and distributed them throughout the second floor, directing them out towards the win-

Rigged by special effects supervisor Thomas Fisher and crew, the fifteen-foot motorcycle jump into the flood control channel was performed by stuntman Peter Kent. Support wires were removed from the footage via computer graphics.

The Cyberdyne building erupts in flames. More than one hundred gallons of gasoline were detonated electronically to produce the massive explosion.

dows. At the same time we detonated the windows—which were real tempered glass—we detonated the cans of gasoline to create the huge fireball. The idea was to make it look like the explosion itself was blowing the windows out."

Seven cameras recorded the explosion from several different angles. "Everybody moved completely away from the building when we shot it," said Ling. "The blast not only blew out most of the second floor windows, but all sorts of set decoration upstairs went out the windows as well. Gas ignites and dissipates very quickly, however; so even though it created a huge fireball, it did very little damage. A portion of the third floor facade that we had built was burned a little; but other than that, everything went off very well."

Trapped by the SWAT team inside the burning building, Sarah and John make their escape when the Terminator—who has commandeered a SWAT van—crashes into the lobby. "We did two takes on that," recalled Ling. "We had two front window areas built in the lobby with candy glass so the van could crash through easily. The tricky part was getting it to skid just right. Jim wanted to do a hundred-eighty-degree turn, swinging around and jamming up against the hallway, back end first. At first we were concerned that it might skid too much since the floor was highly polished to look like marble. The lobby set was just a facade; and if the van skidded too far, it would break through all of the fake walls we had there. So on the first take we sprayed adhesive all over the floor to create some friction. One of our stunt coordinators, Joel Kramer, drove the SWAT van in, swinging it around and skidding it as he entered the lobby. On the second take it crashed into part of the set and pushed it down the hallway where we had two cameras set up, knocking them over. But we got some good footage out of it. We also had remote cameras set up strategically around the lobby—so we got high angles, side angles, everything."

One of the most elaborate stunts orchestrated during the Cyberdyne shoot was the one in which the T-1000, on a motorcycle, jumps from a second-story window of the building and impacts with a police helicopter hovering nearby. From the beginning, the sequence was intended to be cut together with a combination of live stunt footage, visual effects trickery and stage photography. "Jim realized that this was not a stunt that could be performed safely," said Davis. "Not every director would know that, I might add—some of them believe what they see on the screen. But Jim is a very logical man and he knew from the beginning that he would have to cut that sequence together."

The first part was achieved by harnessing stuntman Bobby Brown so that as he jumped out of the window on the motorcycle, he would be jerked off the bike by a cable and land safely on a pile of boxes. "We cabled him so he wouldn't have to think about jumping off the bike or having it fall on him," said Davis. "The window was rigged to blow out just a fraction of a second before Bobby hit it, and he came out of that window going about thirty miles an hour. Then he flew through the air for about forty-five feet before the cable jerked him off and he landed in the huge pile of boxes we'd put together. It was perfect. Bobby was a two-time world champion high diver and he has great control of his body in the air."

For obvious safety considerations, the police helicopter was not in the shot when the stunt was performed. "We shot the helicopter separately," explained Ling, "and then optically combined it with the shot of the motorcycle stunt. A closeup of the actual impact was shot later on the stage with a mockup helicopter."

After pouring himself through the shattered helicopter cockpit, the T-1000 orders the terrified pilot to jump out of the spinning aircraft. Bobby Brown performed the high fall from the helicopter onto an airbag, as well as a later twelve-foot drop onto the top of a car to complete the sequence. "We jacked up the car," Davis noted, "so that when he hit it, it would drop to the ground, the tires would blow, the doors would fly open and it would look like he had really come down hard. The glass on the windshield broke, too. A twelve-foot fall doesn't sound like much, but it's a long way to fall when you know you're going to land on something hard. Bobby was wear-

In a helicopter, the T-1000 pursues Sarah, John and the Terminator during a harrowing freeway chase. Veteran pilots Chuck and Mike Tamburro performed most of the aerial stunt work.

ing a fall cap on his head, but it flew off and by the time he hit the car it was gone. But he did the stunt perfectly and landed exactly where we wanted him to."

With Sarah, John and the Terminator now in the SWAT van and the T-1000 piloting the helicopter, a major chase ensues on the Los Angeles freeways. Ace pilot Chuck Tamburro executed most of the low-flying helicopter stunts. Closer shots revealing Robert Patrick at the controls were achieved live by suspending a mockup helicopter from a crane attached to a flatbed truck. "The mockup was built by Tom Patterson," said Fisher, "and it had everything on it—functioning propeller and rotor blades and the works. For most of the shots, we took the blades off as a safety precaution since the helicopter was so close to

the van. But the rotor still turned and it looked very realistic. The flatbed truck would drive down one lane of the freeway—out of frame—and the helicopter would hang off the side of the truck over the other lane. The driving motion of the truck made the helicopter look like it was weaving a bit and moving up and down, even though it was just suspended in place. From the camera's point of view, it looked very much like the helicopter was flying."

The T-1000 continues the chase in a liquid nitrogen tanker truck when the helicopter crashes into the back of the SWAT van and is rendered a useless pile of wreckage. With the eighteen-wheeler bearing down on the pickup they have traded for their equally wrecked van, the Terminator smashes the windshield

A stunt double for Schwarzenegger climbs atop the overturned tanker truck as it careens wildly into the steel mill.

from its frame and climbs over the top of the pickup—moving at sixty miles per hour—onto the cab of the tanker truck. At point-blank range, the Terminator launches a grenade into the cab of the tanker. In the explosion that follows, the tanker jackknifes violently and rolls over on its side, sliding into the open doorway of the steel mill. The Terminator rides the side of the truck, jumping off and rolling away a split second before impact.

Jackknifing the 68,000-pound tanker truck so it would roll onto its side and skid proved to be more difficult than anticipated. When repeated attempts to make the truck roll failed, thirty thousand pounds of concrete were added to the top of the tanker. The truck was jackknifed again, and this time it not only rolled but flipped completely over onto its back, tires up in the air. The sequence was eventually cut together using a combination of live-action footage and miniatures.

The Terminator's leap from the truck employed a variety of techniques. "We basically covered the stunt with five pieces of film," said Ling. "The first piece was a closeup of Arnold jumping off with the camera moving on him so it looked like the truck was moving—that was shot stationary with him jumping into a mattress. The second cut was a wider miniature shot of the truck hitting and crashing with a puppet on top—a quarter-scale Terminator puppet which Gene Warren of Fantasy II set up and photographed. Then we cut from that to the 'gyro' dummy, which was a full-size puppet that was curled up into a rolling position and set on a track. We got it rolling and then launched it down a ramp and onto the steel mill floor where it sprang open. From that we cut to a shot of Peter Kent breaking through a railing and landing at the bottom of some stairs. The final shot was of Arnold coming to a stop and getting up."

Throughout the filming of the action-packed *Terminator 2*, major injuries were avoided, largely because of the professional teamwork of Davis and Fisher—and the cooperation of a conscientious director. "Many times we were putting our lives in Tommy Fisher's hands," commented Davis. "There was no avoiding it. I'm not qualified to look at a pyro setup and say, 'This explosion is too big to set a man close to it.' I have to defer to the special effects supervisor. If he says it's okay, I have to trust him. And I do because Tommy knows his job. Plus Jim Cameron is the safest director around doing this kind of action film."

11 December 1990, Fontana, California

The company has moved to another section of the mill. The new area is probably two hundred yards from the totalled big rig still blocking the entryway—it's not even on the same level—but on film it will be just around the corner. For some curious reason, the button on the service elevator says FLOOR 2½—but the elevator rarely works. More often than not, it's seven heartpounding flights of lattice stairs from ground level to the set.

In what had once been the area where molten metal was formed into continuous steel beams, Joe Nemec and his art department crew have erected another giant ladle pouring into a secondary vat aptly designated the "death pit" by cast and crew. Again, the blend of real and unreal is mystifying. One overhead hoist is decidedly genuine; another is lightweight foam rubber. A heavy-duty conveyor leading from the floor to an elevated platform has been fashioned from wood and painted a metallic gray. All of the add-ons are in response to specific story points.

With T-1000 presumably on their trail, the Terminator, Sarah and John Connor emerge from behind the elevator shaft and make their way into the industrial labyrinth of the central platform area. Smoke and sparks are everywhere, and Adam Greenberg's yellow-orange lighting suggests a very real hell on earth. Several takes are needed before the scene is captured satisfactorily by Steadicam operator Jimmy Murro.

While the camera crew prepares for the next shot—which will take the trio past the death pit—Schwarzenegger and Furlong play a game. Standing an arm's length apart, the giant and the boy place hands outstretched in front of them. Staring into each other's eyes, each tries to anticipate his opponent's moves. If one can slap the other's hands before he can react and avoid it, a point is scored. It's difficult to determine who's having more fun.

Cameron watches for a while and sidles over. "Anybody got a quarter?" he asks. A flurry of hands dig into pockets and a quarter is proffered. Cameron places the coin in Schwarzenegger's open palm and then places his own hand—palms up—above the actor's. The two men lock eyes. In a flash, Cameron rotates his hand and plucks the quarter from the actor's open palm before he can react and close his fist. Cameron grins. He tries it again and again he succeeds. A third attempt. Cameron makes his move, but this time Schwarzenegger anticipates it. The snatch is blocked, but the quarter drops through the floor and clinks its way through successive levels of latticework all the way to the ground floor some sixty feet below. "Anybody got another quarter?" Cameron laughs.

A crane-mounted camera records the action as John helps his injured mother to the upper levels of the steel mill during their flight from the T-1000.

MORE IS MORE

T2 It is no surprise that when *Terminator 2* got its official go-ahead, Jim Cameron immediately enlisted the participation of makeup ace and creature creator Stan Winston. Already a veteran of two Cameron blockbusters, Winston had produced prosthetic makeups and animatronic puppets for the original *Terminator* plus a planetful of extraterrestrial lifeforms for the subsequent *Aliens*—earning himself an Academy Award statuette in the process. Having distinguished

himself also on *Heartbeeps*, two *Predator* films and, most recently, *Edward Scissorhands*, Winston was a natural choice to oversee the makeup and animatronic effects for *Terminator 2*.

Cameron's only concern was that Winston, who had in recent years segued into directing with *Pumpkinhead* and *A Gnome Named Gnorm*, might be disinclined to work on a film solely in an effects capacity. Nothing could have been further from the truth, however. "It will never be a case of, 'Well, Stan Winston is directing now, so he doesn't want to do effects anymore,'" Winston asserted. "When Jim approached me to do the creature effects for *Terminator 2*, my answer was an emphatic 'Yes!' I wouldn't want anyone else to do them, in fact, because I feel a pride of ownership in the original *Terminator*. Also, I love working with Jim because he always makes our stuff look terrific. The best our work has ever looked has been in Jim Cameron films."

Although the script was not yet completed at the time Winston agreed to join the production team, he was given a preview in Cameron's living room with the director roughing out the story for him while enthusiastically acting out much of the action. At this point, Cameron projected that Winston's workload on the film would be minimal. The majority of the effects involving T-1000 were slated to be produced using computer-generated imagery. Also, determined not to repeat himself, Cameron did not foresee the need for a terminator endoskeleton in the sequel. All that was to be required of Winston was a series of makeups for Arnold Schwarzenegger that would reveal the progressive stages of damage to the Terminator's outer skin as he engaged in ever-more-violent conflict with his T-1000 adversary.

By the time the script had been fleshed out, however, Cameron and Wisher had written what Winston estimated to be the biggest makeup effects film ever. "Jim came up with just hundreds of insane, impossible effects—which is what he always does. There were

A walking Terminator puppet was engineered by Stan Winston and his creature effects team for use during the Cyberdyne shootout.

Stan Winston studies a bust of Arnold Schwarzenegger sculpted by Shane Mahan. Clay sculptures were a first step in creating the many Terminator puppets required for the film.

more effects in the first two minutes of this script than there had been in the entire first movie! But he had come up with such interesting ideas, we *wanted* to do them. We read the script and got very excited—'Oh! We could do that! Let's do that!' It was scary, because much of it was stuff we had never done before—but that also made it exciting."

An extensive future war sequence in the opening pages of the script which called for multiple terminator endoskeletons accounted for a good portion of the expanded requirements. It was a major change in the approach to the T-1000, however, that would contribute most heavily to the burgeoning animatronics workload. Upon bidding out the numerous computer graphics shots needed to fulfill the script, Cameron and his coproducers had been made painfully aware of the extraordinary cost of that technology. Seeking to alleviate some of that burden, the filmmakers began replacing computer-generated shots with mechanical effects wherever possible. Although a sizable number of computer-generated effects still would be required to effectively create the T-1000 character, the attendant animatronics workload grew and grew.

Before his effects effort got up to full speed, Winston—at Cameron's behest—directed a teaser for the film which Carolco was anxious to disseminate well in advance of the release date. As conceived by Cameron, the minute-long teaser explores a fully automated "terminator factory" of the future. Following an assembly line, the camera reveals the casting and assembly of a chrome endoskeleton, moves on to a machine that fits the skeleton with a fleshlike outer skin and ends with a shot of a completed terminator—Schwarzenegger. "What Jim wanted to tell in the trailer," said Winston, "was that *all* terminators look like Arnold. It was a way to justify Arnold's return in *Terminator 2* after having been destroyed in the first film."

Working within a modest $150,000 budget, Winston avoided costly construction of new mechanical devices as much as possible. The sole original terminator endoskeleton was refurbished, and trick photography and clever cuts were employed to create the impression that multiple versions of it were traveling through the assembly line. Because Winston was able to locate actual state-of-the-art assembly robots, only the skinning machine had to be constructed from scratch. Shot on a small stage at the Hayvenhurst Studios in Van Nuys—one block from Winston's own facility—the teaser was completed in just five days.

With the completion of the trailer, Winston

and his staff of forty-some artists and technicians began producing the numerous prosthetic makeups and animatronic effects required for the film. Included in the prosthetic makeup category were several makeovers of Arnold Schwarzenegger as his character is beaten and shot up during the course of the production. Foam latex wound appliances—sculpted to suggest parts of the chrome endoskeleton revealed underneath—were fabricated and attached to Schwarzenegger's face and body. Prosthetic makeup was also employed to age Linda Hamilton thirty years for the epilogue.

Much more elaborate were the animatronic creations: carefully crafted replicas of the principal performers which were totally artificial, yet brought convincingly to life by puppeteers wielding joystick cable controllers, external rod actuators and radio control devices. Traditionally, the first step in duplicating an actor in puppet form is to take a lifecast of him using an alginate material that sets in approximately twenty minutes. Using

A conceptual drawing by John Rosengrant of the final-stage Terminator makeup. Most of the facial flesh has been torn away, revealing the robotic components underneath. □ A final-stage puppet—complete with endoskeleton—was constructed for a scene in which the T-1000 rams a steel rod through the Terminator's torso.

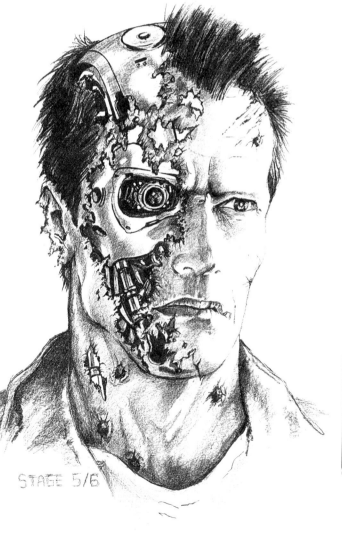

STAGE 5/6

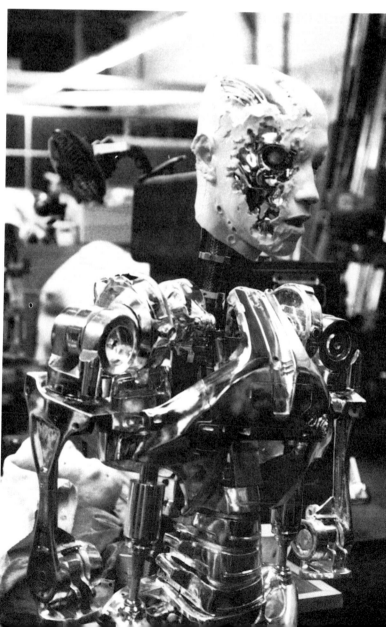

the lifecast as a starting point, refinements in the features and the desired expression are then sculpted in clay. However, for *Terminator 2*, Winston was able to improve on that age-old technique by utilizing a laser sculpting system developed by Cyberware Laboratory.

At the Cyberware facility in Monterey, California, Hamilton and Robert Patrick were scanned by a revolving laser—a process that took only eight to ten seconds per facial scan. The data collected by the laser was then fed into a computer. Using that data, a computer-controlled lathe milled a series of busts of the actors in Styrofoam. Though somewhat crude, these Styrofoam busts were nonetheless more accurate than the likenesses derived from the lifecast technique, which tends to alter the subject's face slightly due to the weight of the alginate. Clay duplicates of the Styrofoam heads were then refined by makeup team sculptors. The rapidity of the laser scan process allowed for a variety of busts to be made—each in the particular expression required for a specific shot. This, too, was an advantage over the lifecast approach, which is usually done in a neutral expression due to the difficulty of holding more animated expressions for long periods of time.

Since the Terminator's expression was generally inert, the traditional lifecasting and resculpting process was employed to duplicate Schwarzenegger. The first such puppet used in the film was needed for a scene in which Sarah and John perform spur-of-the-moment surgery to remove and alter a programming chip buried in the Terminator's head. The puppet head was sculpted in a tilted-down position to approximate the position of Schwarzenegger's head in the live-action as he looked into a mirror and supervised the operation. "Arnold's head needed to be tilted down, with his eyes looking up—as if he was trying to see what is going on in the back of his head. I couldn't just take any Arnold head and then tilt it down and make the eyes look up for this sequence. It wouldn't look right at all, because when you actually assume that pose with your head, many things happen—your brow furrows, the weight of the skin on your neck changes. So that all had to be sculpted into the puppet in the first place." Foam latex was cast up in molds made from the sculpture, and this flexible "skin" was then fitted over a Fiberglas armature that functioned as a skull for the puppet head.

A detailed replica of Schwarzenegger from the waist up was built for a later sequence in which, confronting an entire SWAT team in

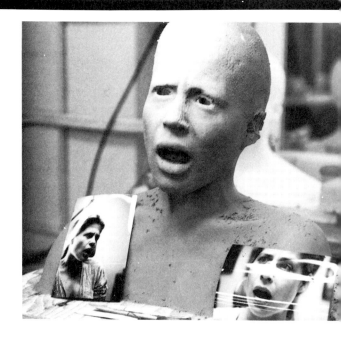

An in-progress clay sculpture of Linda Hamilton by Greg Figiel. A puppet of the actress was needed for a sequence in which Sarah dreams she is engulfed by a nuclear firestorm.

Winston crew members test the Terminator walking puppet in the back of the building shell used for the Cyberdyne exteriors.

the corridors of the Cyberdyne headquarters, the Terminator takes numerous bullet hits to his face and body. Because Cameron wanted to show the cyborg's outer skin tearing away with each hit, the effects obviously could not be achieved using the actor or a stunt double. To effect closeups of the puppet striding through the building, Winston relied on a variation of a technique he had borrowed years before from renowned muppeteer Jim Henson. By positioning the torso puppet over the head of a walking puppeteer, the stride and attitude of the walker would translate directly up to the puppet. "I had used that basic concept to walk the endoskeleton in the original *Terminator*," Winston recalled. "The puppet was placed on a backpack which was worn by Shane Mahan, one of my crew. Shane

would then walk in the attitude that Jim wanted—in this case, a sort of mummylike limp—and the puppet being carried above him looked like it was doing exactly the same thing."

Though the approach was an unqualified success on the first film, modifications were necessary for *Terminator 2*. Unlike the endoskeleton in the original, the puppet in the second film would have to relate sizewise to other actors and set pieces. Positioning it on the shoulders of a grown man—which would place the puppet head nearly ten feet in the air—was clearly infeasible. Retaining the basic kinetic principles of the idea, Winston and his crew devised a walking rig that would allow the puppet to be positioned in front of the operator rather than on his shoulders. "The

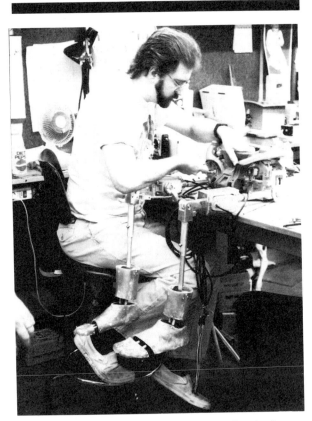

Machinist Craig Caton at work on mechanical Terminator legs for one of the puppets.

Sophisticated engineering produced a puppet armature that precisely duplicated the movements of a human hand.

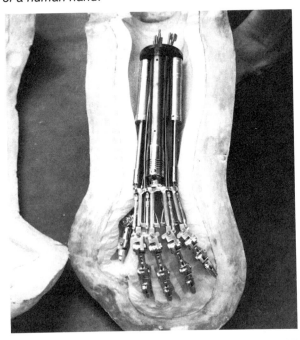

puppet was mounted on a boom arm which was counterweighted to take some of the weight off of the walker, who still carried the puppet and directed the movement. We also had to develop a support system, because this was a big puppet and very heavy. So it was still being carried and moved around by Shane in the harness, but part of the weight was carried by a spring-loaded wheel beneath the puppet." The walking puppet was also equipped with a full range of cable-controlled articulations, including complete spine, head, neck, arm and shoulder movement. Facial expressions were achieved via radio control. Six operators were required to actuate the figure.

Though animatronics technology has become remarkably sophisticated in recent years, much of the ultimate success of the puppet depended not only on its ability to duplicate Schwarzenegger, but Schwarzenegger's ability to duplicate *it*. "Fortunately, Arnold was very good at that. He liked to joke around and have a good time, but when it got down to the nitty-gritty, he was there for us. We duplicated his walk, for example, as closely as we could. But we could only take it so far; and at some point, Arnold had to adjust *his* walk so that it more closely resembled what the puppet was doing. Because he was able to do that so well, it all cut together seamlessly."

One full-length Terminator puppet—articulated from head to toe—was built for a sequence near the end of the film in which the Terminator's body is skewered with a pipe. A minimum of eight puppeteers was required to operate it. In addition, a variety of puppet heads with computerized lip-syncing capabilities were engineered to allow Cameron the greatest flexibility in tying shots of the actor and the puppets together. In addition, unarticulated but still remarkably lifelike Terminator dummies were constructed for falls and stunts that even a trained stuntman could not perform.

All together, more than twenty Terminator puppets were produced for the project. "We made two to four puppets for each stage of the Terminator's disintegration in the film," said Winston. "With that many puppets, we were able to basically match or sync anything

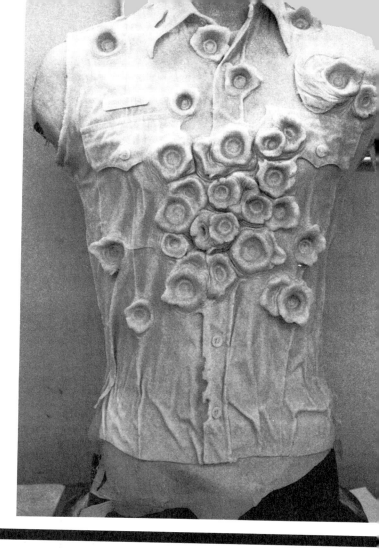

A prototype rubber police shirt—with multiple 'bullet hits'—was constructed for Robert Patrick as the T-1000, but eventually not used in the film.

Arnold was doing in the film—which gave Jim a lot of freedom. To me, the Terminator puppets were not just effects. We had to design and create actual *characters* that had to come in and perform. And not only did they have to perform and react and show expression, they had to do all of that in the same way that Arnold did. I believe these were the best anatomical duplications we've ever produced."

The puppets required to augment the T-1000 transition effects were extremely precise replicas of actor Robert Patrick equipped with some decidedly nonhuman capabilities. Whenever the T-1000 is physically damaged—primarily by weapons fire—its liquid metal core is revealed fleetingly before whatever wounds it sustains heal themselves. To match the liquid-mercury look of the advanced robot being generated via computer animation, it was necessary to bond a high-gloss "chrome" surface onto soft foam latex.

Substantial experimentation with a variety of different materials and processes finally resulted in a realistic-looking chrome finish.

Among the major effects required were T-1000 "body hits"—liquid metal splash holes that suddenly appear when the character is struck by arms fire. "It was like a magic trick—those suddenly appearing flowers," explained Winston. "We used a spring-loaded mechanism with five or six points which folded the piece of chromed foam rubber in on itself. The foam rubber piece was sculpted to look like waves were radiating out from the center—the way mud would look if you shot into it. The mechanism was set up with a radio-controlled trigger that could be operated by the actor. When the trigger was pulled, the mechanism snapped open instantaneously and it looked as if this chrome 'hole' just suddenly appeared." The subsequent effect of the bullet hits closing back up was realized via computer-generated imagery.

The T-1000's fluid nature and its propensity for changing into a variety of shapes and forms required the construction of numerous prosthetic pieces which were attached to Robert Patrick. The most elaborate creation was christened "cleave man"—a shoulder and torso piece used when the T-1000 is split nearly in half by the Terminator, who hits him from behind with a thick metal pole. Because of the T-1000's liquid composition, the pole slices right through his shoulder and upper torso, causing it to separate—but only temporarily—from the rest of his body.

Winston had at first anticipated building a complete articulated body for the effect, but was spared that major undertaking by an ingenious suggestion from Cameron. "Jim came up with the idea of hiding part of Robert Pat-

An early rendering by Shane Mahan for the 'cleave man' effect—one of the T-1000 permutations realized primarily through makeup artistry.

rick's body with a specific camera angle, then attaching a shoulder and torso appliance that could be split open and away from him. It was the kind of suggestion that, as an effects person, I could never have come up with myself, because it meant tying Jim to one particular camera angle—and directors don't like to be locked in like that. But, since it was his idea, it was terrific." Another puppet was employed for a subsequent shot of the T-1000 pulling the bar laterally out of his side.

Aside from prosthetics meant to work in conjunction with Patrick, Winston devised several wholly articulated puppets. One, used fairly early in the film, was used to demonstrate the T-1000's ability to reconfigure after major physical trauma. In the psychiatric hospital, the Terminator fires a point-blank shotgun blast at the liquid metal robot and its head peels open in a wavelike fashion, then reforms with no trace of injury. A mechanical puppet—dubbed "splash head"—was rigged to spring open and later reform via computer animation.

Most of the other puppets were employed in the steel mill battle at the end of the film. For a shot in which Sarah fires a shotgun at her would-be assassin, Cameron wanted a hole blown right through the T-1000's head which would then heal up in moments. An articulated puppet—"donut head"—was constructed with a gaping chrome tunnel that passed through the character's right eye and out the back of his head.

Later in the sequence, the T-1000, having been hit with a grenade, was to splay out in all directions and then plummet into a pit of molten steel before it can recover and reform. This "pretzel man" effect required three stages of puppets. The first was an almost-human form that was mechanized to split open by a spring-loaded trigger. The second was an articulated version of the split-open body trying to reform itself via cable-controlled movement requiring several operators working from beneath. Finally, the sequence utilized a third dummy puppet for the shot of it falling into the vat of white-hot molten steel.

Stan Winston calculated that three hundred makeup and animatronic gags were realized

A conceptual drawing by Mark McCreery of the splayed puppet character required for a sequence in which the T-1000 is hit with a grenade.

The articulated 'pretzel man' puppet being readied for the T-1000's fall into the vat of molten steel.

The 'donut head' puppet—an exacting replica of Robert Patrick—was used for a shot of the T-1000 moments after taking a close-range shotgun blast to the head.

for *Terminator 2*, making it the most ambitious effects film in his company's history. The success of the effort was due, in large part, to the wealth of experience his seasoned crew members brought to the project. "Each film is research and development for the next," Winston concluded. "With *Terminator 2*, we were able to bring all the knowledge and experience gained in the five years since *The*

Terminator into the project, which meant that we could give the audience that much more. People always say that they hope the sequel will be as good as the original. But as filmmakers, we hope to make the sequel *better* than the original—to do everything we did before, but more, bigger, better. We have to forget the statement that 'less is more.' In effects, at least, *more* is more."

16 January 1991, Lake View Terrace, California

What's wrong with this picture?

For the past three months, Linda Hamilton has taken a leave of absence from femininity. Outfitted in black commando gear and toting high-tech combat weaponry, the petite actress has been barely recognizable under a patina of sweat and grime and blood as her character has faced terrible obstacles to protect her young son and the future of mankind.

But today she has a new look. Radiant in a satin nightgown, she sits in a column of warm sunlight streaming in through a window overhead. Her makeup is impeccable. Every hair is in place. Forget that the bed she is sitting on is a no-frills bunk, that the walls of her closet-size room are barren except for a stainless steel mirror and that the tiny window has an offputting crisscross of steel over it. After five weeks in a filthy steel mill, anything is an improvement.

Opposite her is Michael Biehn, wearing the same trenchcoat and tennis shoes that his character—Kyle Reese—had appropriated from a department store shortly after arriving stark naked from the future to save Sarah Connor from a cyborg hitman. Aside from a stubbly beard and a haggard countenance, Reese looks pretty good—considering he was killed in the first film.

This must be a dream.

In fact, it is. The company is shooting in the Lake View Medical Center nestled within the suburban community of Lake View Terrace northeast of Los Angeles. Damaged by a severe earthquake shortly before its dedication, the facility was subsequently deemed unsuitable for its intended purpose and has since served intermittently as a filming location for television and movies. Under the auspices of Joe Nemec, the two-story structure has been surrounded by an uninviting chain link fence topped with coils of concertina wire. A guard shack has been constructed at the gate and a security tower has been erected atop the building. Lake View Medical Center is now Pescadero State Hospital for the Criminally Insane.

It is here that Sarah Connor—deemed dangerously disturbed because of her militant insistence that Judgment Day is only six short years away—is incarcerated and subjected to forced drug therapy and psychiatric treatments. The scene being filmed is the preamble to Sarah's Armageddon dream in which she envisions Los Angeles being obliterated by a nuclear firestorm. In her sleep, she is visited by her dead lover who remotivates her and insists that she has the power to remake the future. It is a tearful, emotional scene—an opportunity for Hamilton to do something other than run and shoot.

Room 19—Sarah's—has been carved out of a somewhat larger room off the main hospital corridor. Cheerfully wallpapered surfaces have been covered over with sterile white panels and a drop ceiling has been added to make the chamber seem even more claustrophobic than it is. One of two "wild" walls has been removed, and from its vantage point camera equipment and lights face in on the tiny set. Mineral-oil smoke has been pumped into the room and the corridor outside to impart a dreamlike quality to the proceedings.

There is more than smoke in the air, however. Just minutes before, word had filtered onto the set that the United States was at war in the Persian Gulf and that targets in Iraq and Kuwait were being severely pounded in the first wave of a multinational aerial assault of staggering proportions.

Work continues unabated, but the mood is somber. Jim Cameron talks quietly with his actors while final preparations are made for the upcoming scene. Once everything is set, the director assumes his customary position in front of the ever-present video cart. Cameras roll and he calls action.

It is near the end of the scene. Having reaffirmed their love, Sarah clings desperately to Reese, covering his battle-weary face with kisses and tears. She begs him not to leave her. She knows what must be done, but she hasn't the strength to do it on her own.

Reese, of course, cannot stay. "Remember the message," he tells her with tender forcefulness. "The future is not set. There is no fate but what we make for ourselves." Cut.

Cameron confers with his actors, offering suggestions for fine-tuning their performances. A second take is ordered, then a third. Satisfied, the director calls for the next setup and a squad of crew members appears on the set and begins repositioning lights and cameras—even the walls.

Those not directly involved gather in small groups to share the latest tidbits of information from the Middle East. A Sony Watchman—part of the Steadicam rig—is pressed into service, tuned in to one of the networks where the President is making a live address to a nation now at war. On the set, it is almost eerily quiet as men and women go about their jobs engrossed in practiced tasks and private thoughts.

The next scene is Michael Biehn's last for the day—and

for the film. Shot from inside the room, he steps through the open doorway and pauses to look back. "There's not much time left in the world, Sarah." He moves into the hallway and is swallowed up by the smoke.

The irony of the doomsday message is lost on no one— most especially Jim Cameron, who confides that he has a younger brother in the marines stationed with U.S. ground forces on the itchy border between Saudi Arabia and Iraq.

Incarcerated at the mental hospital, Sarah has a
dream in which she is visited by Kyle Reese. In a cameo
reprise, actor Michael Biehn returned as the future
warrior who had given his life for Sarah in the first
film. □ Featured also in the dream were graphic
images of nuclear devastation created in miniature
by 4-Ward Productions.

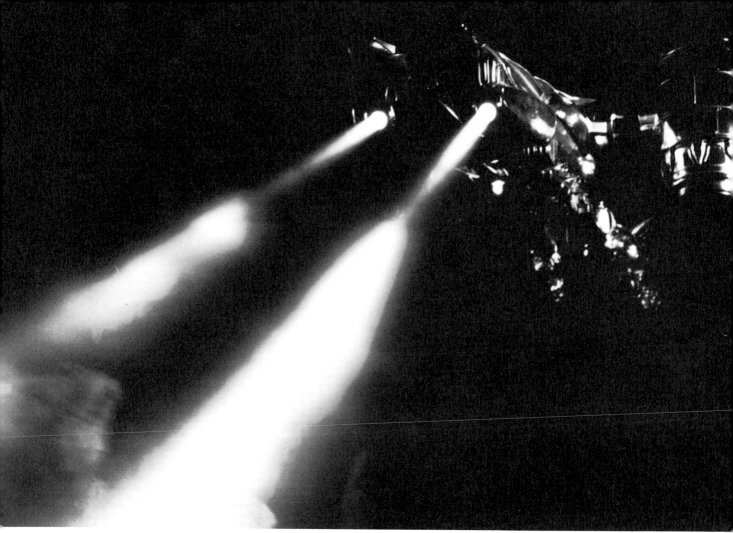

An aerial Hunter-Killer hovers over the battlefield in a future war prologue featuring numerous effects shots accomplished in miniature by Gene Warren of Fantasy II. □ Hunter-Killer tanks rumble across the wasteland of Los Angeles in search of human survivors still waging guerrilla warfare against the machines.

CHAPTER 8

TRICKS AND
MORE TRICKS

They were imaginative, exciting concepts—a mechanism of liquid metal that could transform into any shape; a future war fought by automated, technically-sophisticated machinery; a vision of Los Angeles hit by a nuclear blast; cyborg characters submerged into hot molten steel. The human drama of *Terminator 2* was compellingly supported by literally hundreds of startling visual effects. Conceiving those effects had been relatively easy. Realizing them on the screen was not.

In fact, the effects assignment for the film was so challenging that it was ultimately divided among three visual effects facilities, all of which had worked successfully with James Cameron before. Fantasy II, under the leadership of Gene Warren, was commissioned to create miniature effects for the future war sequence that opens the film; 4-Ward Productions, headed by Robert Skotak and Elaine Edford, took on Sarah's nightmarish vision of a nuclear attack and provided credibility-enhancing closeups of the molten steel effect; and Industrial Light and Magic, with veteran effects ace Dennis Muren supervising, was assigned the numerous computer graphics shots depicting the transformations of the T-1000.

Fantasy II was a logical choice to take on the opening sequence since they had created the similarly conceived future war scenes in *The Terminator*. Though Warren and his team had pulled off the original's effects with great style—especially considering their shoe-string budget—both Warren and Cameron were determined to "do it right" the second time around. "This time there was more money," said Warren, "so we could improve on the things we had never been satisfied with in the first film."

One of those improvements was to increase the size of the models used in the sequence—the Hunter-Killer tank and the aerial Hunter-Killer. By enlarging the machine warriors fifty percent, greater detailing was possible which allowed Cameron to feature the models more prominently. "In *Terminator 2*," said Warren, "Jim really wanted to get in close on the models. So they had to look good enough to hold up to that kind of scrutiny." Because of the change in scale and the determination to improve upon their appearance, none of the models from the first film were usable except for the stop-motion Terminator endoskeleton which was incorporated into the sequel's battle scenes. Warren and his crew had to start virtually from scratch.

Cameron himself had designed the Hunter-Killers for *The Terminator* and, except for minor alterations, those designs were adhered to in the construction of the models for *Terminator 2*. Both the HK tank and the aerial HK were built in approximate fifth-scale out of Fiberglas and vacuformed plastic, then chromed to give them a realistic machinelike texture. "In the first film," Warren noted, "we had just painted the models with a silver automotive paint. That was fine for models in the background; but since these new ones were going to be shown in closeup, they had to look much more believable. We chromed them, then added subtle painted effects to make them look like they'd been through a war."

When completed, the fifth-scale tank was four feet tall, five feet long and weighed almost two hundred fifty pounds. Equipped with four moving treads, the tank was powered by a rheostated cable that could propel the tank forward as well as effect turns by the slowing down or speeding up of individual treads. The tank was also fitted with radio-controlled components, including guns, a moving turret head and searchlights.

To allow for scenes of the aircraft crashing, three aerial HKs were built. Smaller than the HK tank, the aerial HKs were equipped with radio-controlled xenon lights and flown primarily on wires. Some of the more intricate maneuvers, however, necessitated a computerized motion control setup that allowed model and camera moves to be recorded and repeated precisely for shots requiring a layering of effects elements.

The Fantasy II team also recreated the "arrival" effects that they had realized in the first film—shots of the Terminator materializing into the present after his passage through time. Though the effect was to closely resemble the "field of electricity" imagery of the original, it was finessed and improved upon for *Terminator 2*. "First there is an energy vortex," said Warren, "and a kind of translucent Terminator appears inside it. Then there is a full

image with the Terminator dropping to the ground. Jim wanted the image to warp a little bit as the Terminator materialized. It was a simple effect, a cross-dissolve enhanced with animation to produce the electrical look."

Though most of their work on the film was a kind of "*Terminator* revisited" affair, Fantasy II also stepped in to provide miniature shots of the liquid nitrogen truck crashing into the steel mill. A thirteen-foot-long tanker truck made of Fiberglas and vacuformed plastic was built for the sequence, as well as a ten-foot-tall replica of the steel mill exterior. "The miniature set was built on a seventy-five-foot-long platform that was raised about two feet in the air so that we could more easily track and dolly with the camera," said Warren. "We shot the miniature tanker rolling over and then the action of it sliding into the steel mill with the Terminator on top. We built a puppet of Arnold that was radio-controlled so that we could move him a bit as he rode the tanker. We also radio-controlled the front wheels of the truck to get some movement out of them. For the actual slide into the plant, we pulled the tanker by cables that were hidden under the miniature set."

While Fantasy II labored to complete their hands-on miniature shots, Dennis Muren and the ILM computer graphics division were working in the realm of the intangible. Their only "models" were those they had created digitally on a computer monitor. Though computer graphics had been featured in a number of recent films, the still relatively new technology had never been utilized as extensively as it was in *Terminator 2*. "Considering how new the technology is," commented Muren, "it was quite a risk to attempt to create so much of the T-1000 character with computer graphics. Jim was willing to take that great risk. We ended up with fifty-some shots—which is an incredible number of computer-generated shots in a film—but it was really the only way to do what Jim had envisioned with the character. When I saw the storyboards, my first reaction was, 'There is nothing in the world like this.' The effects were so incredible, they couldn't have been done any other way."

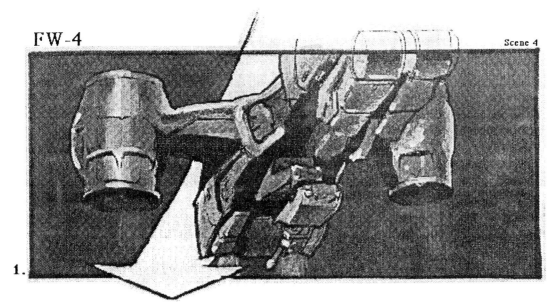

FW-4

Scene 4

1.

UP ANGLE ON FLYING HK CRUISING OVERHEAD...

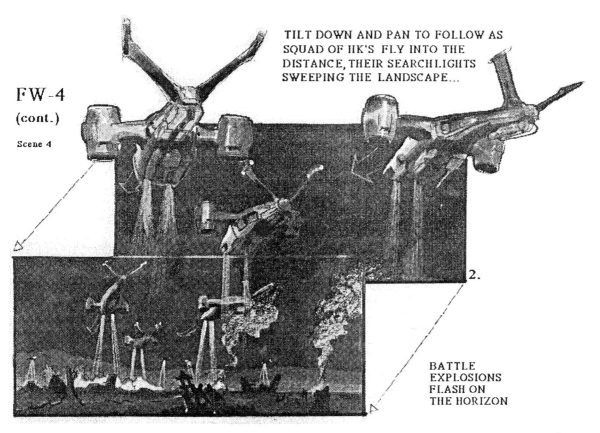

FW-4
(cont.)

Scene 4

TILT DOWN AND PAN TO FOLLOW AS
SQUAD OF HK'S FLY INTO THE
DISTANCE, THEIR SEARCHLIGHTS
SWEEPING THE LANDSCAPE...

2.

BATTLE
EXPLOSIONS
FLASH ON
THE HORIZON

As with other effects scenes in the film, the future war was carefully storyboarded well in advance of production. An early version of the script had a much more expansive future sequence which culminated with a scene inside the time displacement chamber used to send Reese and the Terminator into the past.

Members of the 4-Ward Productions effects crew—under supervisors Robert and Dennis Skotak—survey the damage they have wreaked on an eighth-scale freeway overpass demolished as part of Sarah's nuclear war dream.

Fortunately, Muren and ILM had created similar effects for *The Abyss* just two years before taking on the *Terminator 2* project. For that film, they had computer-generated the pseudopod water tentacle that explores the undersea Deepcore oil rig. "The pseudopod looked really amazing," Muren said, "but that was only one trick. *Terminator 2* required tricks and more tricks. So it was quite a bit beyond what was done in *The Abyss.*"

The computer graphics team began by breaking down their more than fifty shots into categories—easy, moderate, difficult and miraculous. Reference material was shot for each sequence that featured a computer-generated version of the T-1000. "We would shoot Robert Patrick actually going through the action, and then we would reshoot the scene without him to use as a background

plate into which we could put our computer-generated character. It was very helpful to have Robert's performance as a guide, rather than depending on the aesthetic decisions of an animator to create the character's action."

Each T-1000 transformation involved five stages: Stage 1 was a chromelike blob of indistinct shape; Stage 2 was an almost-human chrome form; Stage 3 more closely resembled the actor; Stage 4 was a highly detailed, chrome replica of Robert Patrick; and Stage 5 was his actual live-action image. The first four stages were achieved by "building" appropriate digitized models in the computer, using commercial as well as customized software. "We have software that enables us to build a wire-frame model, starting with a spine. Over that spine we put a series of surface plates, then a kind of 'skin' that smooths over the

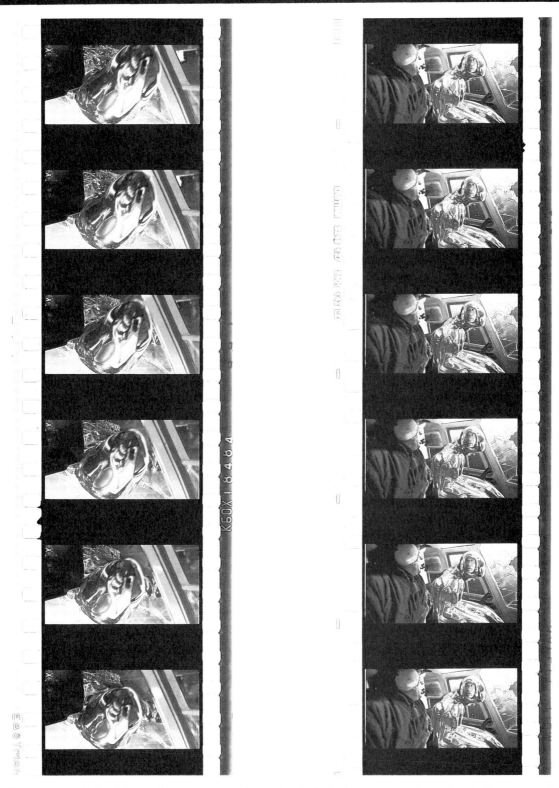

The T-1000—in liquid metal form—pours through a hole in the canopy of a police helicopter and assumes human shape in the seat next to the terrified pilot. The T-1000 shape-shifting effects were computer-generated by Industrial Light and Magic under effects supervisor Dennis Muren.

plates. We use a software program to give that skin whatever look we want—in this case, the look of chrome." Once a basic model was achieved, subsequent stages of the character were built from it. "Each stage was based on the previous one, so we didn't have to build a whole new model for every stage. We built the Stage 2 first and then the Stage 4. The Stage 3 was an interpolation of those two." A technique called "morphing"—which had been developed by ILM for a transformation sequence in *Willow*—was used to smooth out the transformations from Stage 4 to 5 by digitally averaging the two distinct images.

By far the most challenging computer-generated model was the fourth-stage chrome replica of Robert Patrick. To precisely duplicate the actor in digital form, the computer graphics team first stripped the actor down to swim trunks, painted a grid on his body, then photographed him running through the various actions that the fourth-stage T-1000 would have to perform. "We studied his form, just to see how his body parts moved around. Then, in the computer, we made a skeleton. It looked like a real skeleton, with bones and everything. It was never meant to be used in the final form, but it was important in helping animator Steve Williams understand the shape and physical dynamics of the subject. Once we had a handle on that, we were able to build the wire-frame spine and the musculature and the skin."

To duplicate facial features, Patrick's head was laser-scanned at the Cyberware Laboratory in Monterey, California and the data obtained was used to computer-sculpt a small bust of the actor in Styrofoam. "We had a software program that interpolated that data back to a 3-D model shape in our computer," said Muren. "The facial image still had to be fixed up quite a bit by hand because there were shots that were really tight in on the character and the Cyberware bust was not detailed enough. Since the T-1000 was chrome, it wasn't too much of a problem. If we'd been trying to duplicate a person with real human skin, it would have been impossible. We're just not at that point yet with computer graphics."

Working almost to the last minute before the film's release, the ILM computer graphics crew delivered an array of fantastic transformational imagery. "The hardest thing about our work in *Terminator 2*," Muren observed, "was that the computer images had to look absolutely real, not like something that came out of a computer. *And* they had to be at the quality and resolution of the movie film. It takes a lot of computer power to be able to make something that will hold up like that. Fortunately, ILM had recently made a big investment in computer graphics. Shortly before we got the *Terminator 2* assignment, we had added more than $2 million in hardware and software to the department and we had nearly tripled the size of our crew."

While the computer graphics effort for *Terminator 2* had required the talents and expertise of a crew numbering more than forty people, two of the film's most expansive effects sequences—Sarah's dream of the coming nuclear war and the overflowing molten steel in the steel mill—depended on a much smaller team headed by brothers Robert and Dennis Skotak of 4-Ward Productions. The nuclear dream, in particular, relied primarily on miniatures and effects, with very little live-action footage to support it.

The Skotaks began their assignment by viewing footage of actual nuclear detonations and movie simulations. "We looked at everything from *Invasion U.S.A.* to *The Day After* to a 'best of nukes' tape that Jim put together for us," noted Robert Skotak. "We saw footage of just about every atomic test ever recorded. Most of it was out in the desert. What had to be done for *Terminator 2* was transfer that kind of imagery to an urban environment. We've never really seen a nuclear shock wave travel through an environment that everyone is familiar with—a city with skyscrapers and houses and trees and a freeway—and show what would happen to it in a few split instants if it were ever hit with a nuclear explosion."

For one shot, live-action footage of a location overlooking downtown Los Angeles was photographed. "The area had a lot of trees around it, but you could see downtown L.A. with all the skyscrapers in the near distance. We shot plate footage of the location at two different times of day so that we had two very

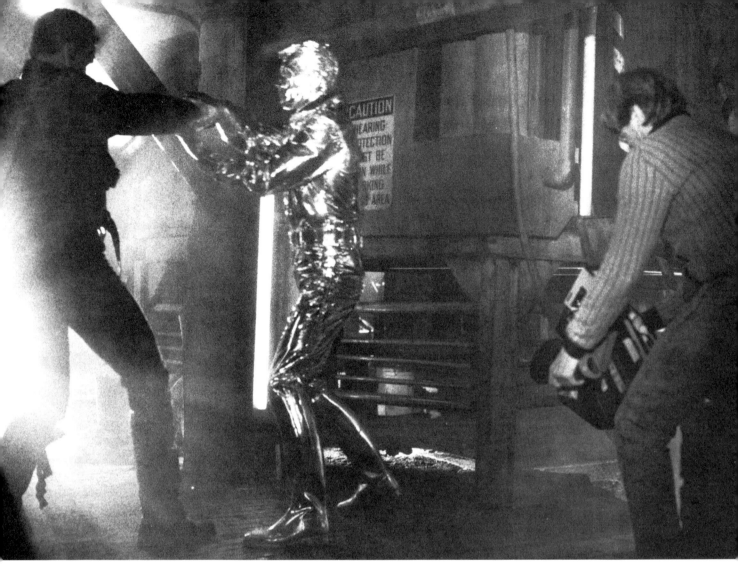

To assist ILM in creating convincing computer animation for the liquid metal T-1000, reference footage was taken of a live performer wearing a reflective mylar suit.

different kinds of light in the sky. One was early in the day when the buildings were broadly lit and the other was at sunset when everything was more backlit. In the initial blast shot we began with the early day footage, then created a flash effect that wiped out the frame and at the same time dissolved from the daylight footage to the sunset footage. So, basically, we used the sun itself to simulate the lighting of a nuclear blast."

After the skyline shot, the sequence continues with a high-angle view of a nuclear shockwave radiating through an urban area, destroying everything in its path. "We shot a still plate of the urban area, then generated a matte painting of Hiroshima-like ruins and produced a kind of sophisticated 'wipe' between the two utilizing a number of two-hundredth-scale breakaway buildings that we blasted with an air cannon and shot high-speed. That footage was used as an element on the leading edge of the wipe so that as the shockwave came across, those buildings disintegrated. So the shot involved a still photograph of the city, a matte painting of the city in ruins, many miniature breakaway buildings to kind of bridge the two and some rotoscope animation."

For subsequent street-level shots of skyscrapers and buildings collapsing, a twen-

A nuclear blast radiates out from ground zero as Los Angeles is decimated in one of Sarah's fearful dreams—a storyboard sequence achieved on film by 4-Ward Productions.

Additional storyboards depict the nuclear shock wave obliterating business district skyscrapers.

tieth-scale miniature city set was built. "We set the vertical structures on their sides facing up so that we could blast primer cord, air cannons and effects fans across them and have it look as if the force was moving in from the side. The buildings all had breakaway surfaces so they would crumble easily." Streetlights, telephone poles and trees were constructed with pivot points near their bases that allowed them to bend and twist when hit with the primer cord blast. "They were quite flexible so they could bend very far, just like the trees you see in atomic test footage."

To set the nuclear explosion firmly in urban Los Angeles, Cameron had conceived of a trademark freeway overpass impacted by the nuclear blast. "We built a fifty-foot by thirty-foot set of the freeway in eighth-scale," noted Skotak. "Many of the vehicles had to be constructed as breakaways, with roofs caving in and doors flying open and windows blowing out. We put primer cord under the freeway to make the pavement stutter and jump."

In addition to realizing Sarah's vision of nuclear holocaust, the Skotaks applied themselves to creating a realistic molten steel effect for the steel mill sequence near the end of the film. Although most of the "background" molten steel shots were photographed live at the Fontana location, the Skotaks were charged with developing a technique that would allow for credible closeups of the fiery liquid. "Our molten steel shots were to be closer-up versions of the live-action shots specifically meant to really sell the idea of the molten steel flowing out of the untended ladle and onto the floor."

After many tests, the Skotaks came up with the idea of shooting a white paint mixture as it poured from a quarter-scale ladle onto a miniature set. "We were able to pull a matte off of that image and then print it several times brighter so that it became luminous, rather than looking like flat white paint. We wound up with what was essentially liquid light. Then we added graded mattes to that image to give it an orange-ish glow."

Long after principal photography wrapped in late March, the Skotak brothers, Dennis Muren, Gene Warren and their respective crews continued to labor over the more than one hundred fifty effects shots crucial to telling the *Terminator 2* story. Whether transforming the T-1000 from a mass of amorphous liquid chrome to the image of a handsome cop or creating a nuclear explosion or simply supplying five seconds of miniature photography to help sell an action sequence, the visual effects in *Terminator 2* played an integral role in making the filmmakers' vision a cinematic reality.

6 March 1991, Valencia, California

After more than a hundred days of shooting, principal photography is nearing completion and spirits are up.

Exactly four months from the time the exteriors for the shootout at Cyberdyne Systems were filmed in San Jose, cast and crew have assembled at Stage 8 of the Valencia Studios just thirty miles north of Los Angeles where the Cyberdyne interior has been constructed. It is here that the Terminator, Sarah and John, led by computer scientist Miles Dyson, come to destroy the research that would ultimately lead to Skynet and the near annihilation of the human race.

As conceived and realized by the art department, the laboratory is a cold, metallic labyrinth of computer technology in clean grays and whites. Blue-green emergency lights—presumably set off by the intruders—flash ominously over an array of computer consoles. Violet fluorescent lights cast eerie lavender reflections off chrome and glass. Except for a three-foot-long inflatable dinosaur hanging incongruously from the ceiling, the split-level main room and attendant offices are a study in high-tech efficiency.

But today the crew is intent on wreaking havoc in this ordered environment. Being readied is a series of shots in which Dyson and his cohorts race against the imminent arrival of the police to complete their search and destroy

mission. Disk holders and files are thrown to the floor; computer consoles are smashed beyond redemption. One crew member wheels an unsuitably intact console to the edge of a small stairway, unceremoniously pushes it off, then smiles and says, 'New technique.' It works. The prop is now battered and broken into several pieces.

There is an unmistakable air of frivolity in this demolition derby. The crew takes a none-too-subtle glee in what they jokingly refer to as 'hammer time.' "Hammer time!" is called and crew members bring out hammers and begin to pummel the set with relish. "Linda Hammer-time," says one, playing on the name of star Linda Hamilton. "Oscar Hammer-time," says another. The jocularity is in sharp contrast to earlier days on the set, some of them grim times sweating at the bottom of a flood control channel or eating dust at an abandoned steel mill.

Outside, too, spirits are high. Arnold Schwarzenegger's assistant energetically rides a Lifecycle stationed next to the actor's trailer; Eddie Furlong amuses himself with a new camera; crew members laugh at a sign posted above a lightboard which states: "If assholes could fly, this place would be an airport." Some wear homemade badges depicting a bone with a red slash through it—a graphic representation of a phrase that

has caught on with cast and crew: "Don't bone me." Each time something runs afoul, at least one crew member can be heard saying, "Uh-oh—boned again." Laughter inevitably follows. Everyone is jovial. The shoot is almost over.

Cameron sits calmly and watches as the set is ransacked and lights are added to this corner or that. After an hour of frenzied activity, everything is readied and Hamilton, Schwarzenegger, Furlong and Joe Morton—the actor playing Dyson—are summoned to the set. When they arrive, Cameron calls for a rehearsal, stationing himself behind a video monitor and yelling "Action!" through a megaphone. A Steadicam traverses the room as Sarah hurriedly carries a box of files toward a heap on the floor that will later become a massive bonfire; the Terminator delivers powerful blows to the computers with an ax, then relinquishes the weapon to Dyson so that he may take a less effectual, but satisfying whack at the monster of his own creation. Cameron yells "Cut!" He confers briefly with the Steadicam operator and the sequence is rehearsed again. Four run-throughs are required before the action and camera angles are finessed to the director's satisfaction. The sequence is finally shot without incident and, with the exception of Hamilton, the actors return to their trailers to wait out the next long setup. On his way out,

Schwarzenegger passes a writer leaning against a wall with a notebook in her hands. He suddenly stops, grabs the notebook, reads a word or two written there, then hands it back. "Just wanted to make sure you spelled my name right," he jokes.

While crew members prepare for the next shot, Hamilton and Cameron meet at a video monitor to view a rough cut of the theatrical trailer for *Terminator 2*. The preview is breathtaking, heartstopping and Hamilton is impressed. "It's awesome," she says. "Yeah,"

Cameron responds, somewhat irritably. "Now if we could just get it done and into the theaters so people will come and see this movie." He hurries off and one is reminded that, for him at least, the ordeal is far from over.

The Terminator spearheads the mayhem at Cyberdyne and its doomsday databanks are systematically destroyed. The high-tech computer lab was one of the few studio sets constructed for the film.

YOUR BASIC LOGISTICAL HELL: AN INTERVIEW WITH JAMES CAMERON

T2 *Let's talk about shooting the film. You started on location near Lancaster, shooting the scenes at Salceda's desert camp. Did it take some adjustment time for everyone to get back into the* Terminator *mode?*

No. It was as if six years hadn't passed. Arnold stepped right into the character, and Linda was totally in shape, totally prepped for it. Obviously it was the shakedown period for Eddie, to see how he was going to do; to see if the crew and all of those lights were going to inhibit him. They didn't affect him at all. He was fine. So we got off to a good start.

You shot for several weeks in the flood control channels all around Los Angeles County. Where did the idea for a canal chase come from?

It's something I'd wanted to do for a long time. I like the "no escape" metaphor. On a roadway, you always feel like you can turn off. But in a canal, there's no exit. You're like a rat in a maze. You can't get out. And the ultimate version of that idea is a kid on a little dirtbike being chased by this huge block of steel that completely fills the canal behind him like a piston in a cylinder. We never found a canal that was as narrow as I would have liked—I wanted that truck scraping both walls as it came through.

What were the difficulties of shooting in a canal?

One of our biggest limitations was that the entrances and exits were few and far between. So we had to get our vehicles and equipment into the canal sometimes miles away from

The Terminator defends his young charge.

Cameron inspects a weapon on the set of
Salceda's training camp.

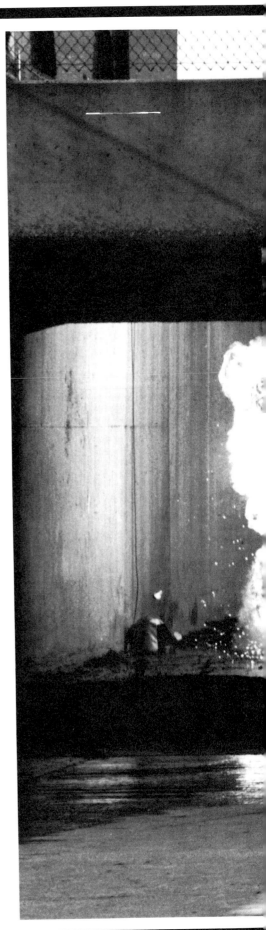

The Terminator escapes with John as the pursuing
tow truck rams a concrete column and explodes.
Cameron had long wanted to film a chase in the
Los Angeles canal system.

where we were actually shooting. It was your basic logistical hell. Another problem was that the canals were coated with green algae on the bottom, which made them extremely slick. We couldn't even walk down there. We had to clean them with high-pressure water jets and dam the water. It turned into a whole hydro-engineering project—which caused the first of many *Abyss* flashbacks.

The canal chase—like so many of the action sequences in your films—has a random, almost haphazard quality. What is your approach to shooting action scenes?

There is a sense of reality and immediacy that I strive for. In the canal chase there wasn't a single shot where the camera was stationary, except for when Arnold's motorcycle jumped off the side—and that was a deliberate rest note that I felt was needed in the middle of all the high-speed action. When I shoot action sequences, I make a conscious stylistic decision to create mayhem. But mayhem can't come from mayhem—it has to come from extreme organization.

Do you storyboard your action sequences?

Only if there are going to be other elements added to the shot or if I need to communicate something to a second unit director. In general, I find storyboarding action sequences very limiting because they are still-frame versions of something that has to be kinetic. I like to get all the people there and rehearse a sequence and feel the energy of it right there. I can't dissect it that much ahead of time. Of course, stunts involving vehicles and things like that have to be worked out months in advance. But I don't find that storyboards are especially helpful for those shots, either. I prefer to work them out on video.

You have a tendency to keep your second unit footage to a minimum. Why is that?

I just enjoy shooting it myself. I was lucky on this film because Gary Davis was a really excellent second unit director who had a strong sense of what worked kinetically. He saw things very much the way I saw them, and his footage cut in with my footage perfectly. So it was relatively easy to delegate to him.

On location, Cameron and crew choreograph portions of a street chase using model cars and trucks.

At what point do you say to yourself, "Okay, I've got what I need—second unit can take it from here"?

I always categorize shots by priority: These are the shots I absolutely need to tell the story; these are the shots which are slightly lower priority that I need to make the sequence spectacular; and these are the shots I'd love to have if I can get them, just to add detail or clarity to a moment. It's all a question of where you draw those lines. I mean, do I actually *need* a drainage canal chase to tell the story? Of course not. But the audience is coming to be exhilarated, and I aim to do that. The tow truck could have just driven down a ramp to get into the canal instead of crashing into it from a bridge—that would have told the story. But it wouldn't have been a great moment.

So you take care of the first two categories of shots and leave the third for second unit?

Not necessarily. The second unit may very well do a storytelling shot if I'm in the middle of doing something else and the shot is fairly easy and straightforward. Not that they couldn't do a complicated shot—second unit could do anything I could do. They had the same stunt drivers, and Gary Davis was just as good at blocking out action as I was. Delegating to second unit isn't a question of competence or capability—it is always about communication. I have to be able to exactly communicate what I want out of a shot in order to turn it over to them. If I can articulately download to them what I need, they can do it.

The production schedule took you from the canals up to San Jose to shoot the Cyberdyne exteriors. It would seem that, logistically, that must have been one of the most challenging sequences.

It was. I kind of made a meal of the parking lot scene—the Terminator shot up all of the LAPD's rolling stock in about thirty seconds of screen time. I embraced that sequence because it was the first time in the film that you

got a real feeling of this being the Terminator you remembered from the first film—when he comes to town, he brings hellfire. I hadn't really had a chance to do any of that yet. And Arnold needed a kicking-ass fix. We did one shot where he put about four hundred rounds into three different cars and just shot them to pieces. Obviously they were fake—he was firing blanks and the rounds were already in the cars—but it looked like he just mowed down half the parking lot, all in one take. Afterwards, I walked over to him and said, "Now Arnold, you can't tell me that wasn't a rush." And he admitted it was.

One of the major events of the sequence is the Cyberdyne building being blown up. Did that go as planned?

Perfectly. That was one of our most textbook shots. We set up every camera we had so that we wouldn't miss one little detail of the building blowing up—second unit cameras and main unit cameras and even a special camera that was there to do effects photography. Tommy Fisher spent five hours setting up all of the gas mortars. We had a window of time in which we were actually permitted to do the explosion—it had to be late enough that we wouldn't disturb rush hour traffic on the nearby freeway and freak everybody out, and yet early enough not to disturb people's sleep. So it had to be done between ten and midnight and the police had to shut down the two adjacent freeways that were within sight of the building. I set up all the cameras and the extras and the stunt guys in the foreground, choreographed all of that action, and then got in a helicopter and took off to shoot it from the air. It involved calling a bunch of cues, starting one set of cameras at one point and another set of cameras at another point, doing a countdown for the effects guys, and finally cueing them to set off the explosion. It was very, very complicated.

From there you went to the Terminal Island Freeway.

That was more fun and mayhem. We went

from shooting all of these explosions and fire and squibs and tear gas to a state-of-the-art helicopter chase where we were flying a Jet Ranger helicopter on the freeway just one foot off the ground through traffic.

Were you concerned about the dangers involved in shooting the helicopter chase?

Absolutely. You have to find the balance between getting dynamic material and the risk involved in getting it. The stunt pilots, Chuck Tamburro and his brother Mike, were always willing to push further than I was willing to have them go—which is the way it should be. If they said, "This is the line," then I asked them to go not quite to that line. And that is sometimes a difficult thing to do. You're out there on location, directing an action sequence, and maybe you're behind and you have all of this time and money to think about. In those circumstances, it would be real easy to push for it and say, "Just do it." But you have to accept the consequences of something like that. If someone gets hurt in that situation, it's your fault. So I draw those lines very clearly. It's a matter of being able to live with myself afterwards.

After the freeway shoot, you spent about five weeks filming at an abandoned steel mill. What were some of the difficulties involved in creating the illusion of a functioning steel plant?

The biggest mistake I ever made was mixing molten steel with people. We wound up getting some good shots and it looks very much like I imagined it when I wrote it—kind of the pit of Hell. But it turned out to be a very hard thing to do, simulating what is essentially a glowing liquid. It took a lot of research and development to come up with that look.

Had molten steel ever been simulated in a film before?

Not that I know of. There have been other movies that attempted similar kinds of things—*Indiana Jones and the Temple of Doom*, for example, did a lot of stuff with molten magma. But there has never before been the necessity of immersing a human being in molten steel, because that is not physically possible. If it happened, the character would just burst into flame—which is a relatively easy effect. But in this case, it was a complex, interactive sequence. The sad thing is that we spent all of that time and money and, ultimately, it's not that spectacular. The audience will just assume we did it somehow, but it won't impress them because it's kind of a mundane thing. Molten steel, big deal. They'd be impressed by an alien spacecraft, and yet that would really be a much simpler thing to do.

Did you do a lot of research to determine how an actual steel mill operates?

We studied several films that featured the making of steel. The part of the process that seemed the most graphic to me was the moment that the steel pours from one vessel into another, so we wanted to simulate that. In reality, they don't even do that anymore. Now they have a slide gate that opens at the bottom of the ladle, so you would actually see very little of the molten steel as it poured into the slot below. But—as always in moviemaking—the point isn't what something really looks like, but what the audience *expects* it to look like. If it looks the way they imagine it, it is real to them.

You shot the future war sequence not far from the steel mill site. Conceptually, how does the future war in Terminator 2 *differ from what you did in the original film?*

In the first film, the future war was an actual memory of Michael Biehn's character—a specific event that happened to him. In *Terminator 2* it is really just an opening sequence to set the stage for the film. I tried to make it look like documentary footage from World War II. So it contains discordant flashes of information, like a quick documentary of a war that hasn't happened yet.

You often feature dreams in your films, and

*The Terminator at
Cyberdyne—a sequence
which proved to be one of
the most logistically
challenging of the film.*

this one is no exception. What do the dream sequences do for Terminator 2?

The dreams are a way of putting the audience in Sarah's shoes, viscerally, so that they can see the world through the same set of values that she does. Dreams, in general, are very important to me. I think they are as significant as any other part of our daily reality, and certainly an important part of our psychological process. And, personally, dreams have played a crucial role in my creative process. When I was a kid I had a lot of dreams about nuclear wars. I don't know what that says about me, but I'm sure it has impacted on the kinds of films I make.

After filming wrapped, you were left with a very short postproduction schedule. What were the problems entailed in meeting the film's summer release date?

I had about the same amount of time in postproduction for *Terminator 2* as I had on *Aliens.* So I knew that it *was* possible to complete a complex effects film in that amount of time. The most important thing was staying on top of it while we were shooting—editing scenes as they were shot. I just had to realize that I wasn't going to get a day off until the film was in the theaters—that was a given. And that was part of the challenge of making the movie. It was not only a logistically difficult picture, a technically difficult picture and a dramatically ambitious picture, it also had to be done on a ridiculously short schedule. So what else is new?

You have a reputation for being a very tough and demanding director.

Yeah, I know that. It's just part of the working process for me. Some people take it personally and some don't. The ones who work with me again are the ones who don't. They realize that it's just a matter of my trying to keep things moving and keep people on their

A motorcycle-mounted cameraman records the action as the Terminator fires at the pursuing tanker truck from a battered pickup. The safety of the cast and crew was a major concern throughout the action-laden shoot.

Director James Cameron on the set.

Bruised and bloodied, the Terminator, Sarah and John prepare for the final showdown with the T-1000 at the steel mill. Cameron likened the grueling shoot to fighting a war.

toes and thinking. Because I am always thinking ahead—"What hasn't been thought of? What hasn't been prepared? What could throw a monkey wrench into things three setups down the line?" So, yeah, I'm harsh on people because I want to inspire them to do their best and to think things out, not just coast and ask what time lunch is going to be. It's a business, not a party. Every time I start a film I have a fantasy that it will be like a big family and we'll have a good time and we'll have all of these wonderful, creative moments together. But that's not what filmmaking is—it's a war.

And you're General Patton.

Well, I've never slapped anybody—but yeah, it's a war. It's a group of humans fighting against the tendency of the universe to become disorganized. Entropy is there every day, and you're struggling to make something out of it. For me, that's pretty much the filmmaking process in a nutshell.